Vital Signs

A PATHWAY TO CONGREGATIONAL WHOLENESS

Dan R. Dick

DISCIPLESHIP RESOURCES

PO BOX 340003 • NASHVILLE, TN 37203-0003
www.discipleshipresources.org

ISBN 978-0-88177-495-5

Library of Congress Control Number

Vital Signs

TABLE OF CONTENTS

Introduction

The United Methodist Church isn't well. The twentieth century witnessed an almost constant decline in church membership, per member giving, worship attendance, Sunday school participation, mission giving, evangelistic outreach and invitation, and community involvement. Competition from schools, civic organizations, jobs, and leisure activities demanded more and more time, eventually infringing on the sacred space/time of Sunday morning. By the dawn of the twenty-first century, mainline denominations scrambled to claim "market share," to find new and creative ways to entice people to come to church. Having abandoned most of the fundamental tenets of faith, theology, and polity that gave them their identity in the first place, the mainlines churches opted for a more consumeristic, non-demanding, highly entertainment-oriented style of church—jumping on the playing field created by the evangelical/independent "big boys" like Willow Creek and Saddleback. Slowly, but surely, some bright, shining stars appeared in the United Methodist sky— churches that beat the odds, attracting large congregations, piling up impressive giving and attendance statistics, and offering an ever-growing menu of programs and activities. These churches got the job done, becoming the models for the rest of the struggling congregations. Successful pastors presented "you can do it too" workshops, wrote books, produced videos, and literally thousands of clergy and laity leaders from around the world stopped by to visit these showcase congregations. The message is clear: "big is better, success means 'more!'"

However, if this is true, why aren't things getting better? Our numbers, denominationally speaking, continue to decline. With the exception of high-profile crises like tsunamis and hurricanes, our mission giving is embarrassingly low and our per-member giving continues to decrease. Certainly, attendance isn't falling quite as quickly as membership— unless you adjust it against population statistics, then it is pretty pathetic. We have had over a generation of "Seven Keys to . . . " and "Ten Steps to . . ." and "Purpose Driven/Vision Driven/Mission Driven . . ." congregational self-help books that have made little, if any, positive impact on our congregations. It appears that the isolated pockets of booming megachurch success may not be replicable across the larger landscape of United Methodism. The church growth movement, and its many prolific proponents, has defined one kind of church (labeled "successful"). A growing church, conventional wisdom teaches, needs to be culturally savvy, technologically up-to-date, well-marketed, non-threatening, entertaining, and make few, if any, demands on its participants. Generally, it requires a visionary, tireless, charismatic pastor (almost universally male) and a professional Board of Directors and decision makers. A prime location doesn't hurt, as well as a finely cultivated core of "deep pocket" givers. With a good leader, a great location, lots of money, a paid staff, a big marketing budget, a television/radio outlet, state-of-the-art digital technology, and a feel good message, "you, too, can grow a large church."

Consider for a moment, though, that this model of the church might not be the best one. There is nothing inherently wrong with being big, but there is nothing inherently good about it either. King Kong was big—it didn't help in the end. Growth is not necessarily bad; in fact, it is essential for healthy development. But ungoverned, unbounded growth can be deadly, as in the case of cancer. If the true purpose of the church is to serve the needs of the world, then you can never have enough people. But if the purpose of the church is for people to sit in a pew and hear stories about God without any kind of challenge to make a real difference, then one might question the benefit of generating more inert listeners.

It may be that our standards of success—the metrics by which we evaluate the value of the church—are misdirected, or even wrong. It is not that growth isn't a valid measure of success, but that it is not *the* measure of success, nor is it a worthwhile end in itself. Where the formation of faith is concerned and spiritual development and Christian community is the point, qualitative (rather than quantitative) measures are most important. Bigger says nothing about faithful, and active says nothing about effective. The value of our ministry is judged by the impact it makes on people's lives, not by how many people show up.

If size, money, and program are not adequate criteria by which to judge a church's value, then what are? Qualitative evaluation is much more difficult and time-intensive than quantitative evaluation. It is so much easier to count the number of people in worship than to assess what they experienced and how it affects their thinking and behavior. Yet, we are the church, the body of Christ. Unless we understand the impact on individual's lives of our ministries, practices, and shared experiences, we really cannot hope to be effective.

For the past six years[1], I have been visiting, studying, surveying, consulting with, and analyzing over 700 congregations across North America to better understand effective structures, processes, leadership, and systems for spiritual formation and development. With the assistance and cooperation of dozens of District Superintendents, Directors of Connectional Ministry, Bishops, and hundreds of congregational leaders I gathered an incredible body of information on churches of all shapes, sizes, demographics, ethnographics, economic and educational strata, and theological bias. Based initially on the criteria of "growth" (churches with increasing membership, attendance, money, etc. being "healthy;" churches with declining numbers, "unhealthy"), I attempted to divide my sample accordingly. It didn't work.

As I analyzed the gathered data and information I found that many congregations defy a simple labeling of healthy or unhealthy. One church of over 7,000 members struggles to get 800 people to attend on a Sunday morning. A church with a fully funded three-million-dollar budget spends less than 1% on anything other than itself. A fast-declining church of forty-five members feeds over 500 hot meals to the poor and marginalized each week. A church of 300 members, down in four years from almost 700 members, boasts over 400 in worship each week, with less than 2% of their membership inactive. A church of 145 has every member active in Sunday school, an accountability group, and some form of leadership within or beyond the congregation, but has lost over 80 members in three years. These are some of the anomalies that make categorization difficult.

What differentiates these churches from those that fit easily in a "growing" or "declining" category? Pouring through the reports, notes, and surveys, a second set of criteria emerges. This second set of criteria I label "Sustainability," and they measure the overall stability of the congregation for ongoing mission and ministry. Among the measures of sustainability are:

---

1. Beginning in 1999 through mid-November 2005.

Levels of active participation

Accountability for spiritual development

Outward expressions of faith

Standards for membership

Practice of the means of grace

Communal identity

Dependence on pastoral leadership

Awareness of impact of program and ministry

Base of financial and leadership support

Dependence on paid staff

Dependence on location

Clarity of, and commitment to, a shared vision

Hours per week spent in meetings and planning vs. hours spent in formation and service

Percentage of budget spent on maintenance, administration, and overhead vs. amount spent on mission and ministry program

Alignment of activities with values and vision of congregation

Decision-making processes, especially in areas of conflict and contention

Many differences emerge between highly stable and unstable congregations, but these listed are the fundamental points of comparison and contrast. Highly stable congregations establish a strong ministry base that can endure massive upheaval and disruption without losing momentum. In unstable congregations, the change of just one or two contributing factors can undermine the ministry of the congregation and force the congregational leadership to begin building momentum anew.

By integrating the two sets of criteria, both growth and sustainability, four church "types" emerge. Where a congregation is highly stable and growing, vitality exists. This is the optimal situation for any congregation, and the focus of this book. These *vital* churches are rare in The United Methodist Church—

of the 717 congregations included in this study, 69 fell into the vital church category (9.6%). Interestingly, these are not the churches that get a lot of attention.
Occasionally their story is told, but for the most part, the members and leaders
of these churches are too busy doing the work of the body of Christ to teach
workshops, write books, and host seminars. As one vital leader reflected, "The
old saying is, 'Those who can't do, teach.' Well, we're doing, not teaching!" The
growth in vital churches tends not to be dramatic, so they often continue in
faithful service virtually unnoticed, even though they have much to teach the
denomination. They exist in every conference, in every jurisdiction, and their
journey into vitality is remarkably similar. Those common experiences and
attributes combine to create a vision for vitality.[2]

About one-third of the congregations in this study (234, or 32.6%) are experiencing growth, but their sustainability is low. In a living organism, a condition of growth that weakens or diseases rather than strengthens is referred to as
"dystrophy." *Dystrophic* congregations are those where there is growth for
growth's sake (think obesity or cancer) that ultimately makes it harder for the
"organism" to survive. As the church grows bigger and bigger, it requires more
and more money, time, energy, and expertise just to keep the doors open. As
one pastor in a dystrophic congregation lamented, "I work longer and longer
hours to do more and more work that has less and less to do with why I got into
ministry in the first place." Dystrophic congregations accomplish a lot of good,
they touch many lives, they reach many people, but they are very hard to sus-
tain for long periods of time, and they experience an enormous amount of waste
and burnout.

Occasionally, a church goes through a period of numeric decline that
enables it to become more active and effective, rather than less. In biology, when
a complex organism reverts to a simpler form, this is called "retrogression."
Retrogressive congregations are those who have made some hard decisions that
lead to fewer programs, fewer services, a narrower focus, or more specialized
ministry that results in some people leaving the congregation. In many cases,
the decline in active participation results from the core congregation's leadership decision to get serious about membership standards, spiritual formation, or

2. For the purposes of gathering information and receiving the most candid feedback possible, a confidentiality statement was signed with each congregation. No congregations or individuals will be named in this book, though many churches will be readily recognizable through
the general descriptions and specific illustrations. All quotes are verbatim, through interview
notes and digital recording.

Christian service, and the more passive members look elsewhere because the church becomes too demanding. For whatever reason, most retrogressive congregations find themselves more active, more involved, and more effective, though with fewer participants. In this study, fifty-one congregations (7.1%) find themselves in a highly stable, but declining position. An important fact to note is that almost every vital congregation reported a period of retrogression in their journey to vitality. More will be explained about this condition later.

This leaves one last congregational type, perhaps the most disturbing and troubling of all: unstable and declining, or *decaying*, churches. Many people are troubled by the term "decaying" as applied to congregations, but I use the term intentionally for the emotional impact it wields. Most of the congregations in this category (363, or 50.6%) are at the threshold of crisis, whether they acknowledge it or not. Make no mistake, this term is not intended as a value judgment, but as a value-neutral descriptor. A state of decay exists where decline and lack of stability make the organism unsustainable. We have a significant number of congregations in steep decline, deep denial, and dysfunctional stagnation. Pretending it isn't real and it isn't serious is no longer an option.

In all four church types, the grace and love of God can be found. My intention in this book is not to insult or condemn, but to illuminate and challenge. The sample used in this research is not significant; therefore, what I hope to do is raise some key questions, invite people to test for themselves the propositions put forth, and to see how these ideas might help them visualize a future for the church. This is a journalistic rather than scientific report. The validity of the sustainability criteria can only be tested in the laboratory of the congregation.

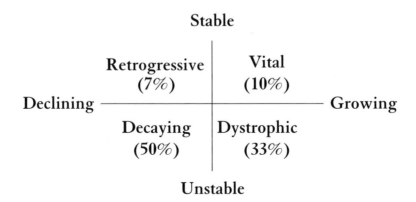

The vision for congregational wholeness presented in *Vital Signs* is predicated on three assumptions:

1. Vitality is a value shared by conference and congregational leaders throughout The United Methodist Church. Everyone would like to see the church both stable *and* growing.

2. While the vast majority of our churches are limited in growth potential, almost every congregation can work to become more stable.

3. God empowers every congregation through the Holy Spirit to become vital, vibrant, healthy centers for Christian discipleship. Every congregation has at least pockets of vitality upon which to build and grow.

Chapters 1 through 4 describe each of the four church types, beginning with the Decaying Congregation, moving through Dystrophic Congregations, to Retrogressive Congregations, before examining the Vital Congregation. Each church type is presented as a general descriptive category. I am not presenting what ought, or ought not, to be, but a description of what is. Many people have attempted to "correct" my perceptions, redefining a dystrophic church as a vital one, simply because they do not like the title. But the category labels reflect how a church "scores" on the criteria for growth and sustainability. Each congregation self-scored, locating itself in one of the four types. These four types are nothing more than a conceptual frame (it is not my desire to stick anyone in a box or slap a label on them) that differentiates a growing and stable reality from the three others.

Each of the four church types will be described using fifteen criteria:

1. sense of identity

2. shared clarity of purpose

3. focus of the congregation

4. awareness and understanding of God's vision for the church

5. governing and guiding values

6. impact awareness

7. leadership

8. the role of the appointed pastor(s)

9. programmatic design

10. organizational structure

11. money

12. the role of worship in the life of the congregation

13. the role of education in the life of the congregation

14. the congregation's relationship to the community

15. the congregation's relationship to the connectional system

Chapter 5 examines the Pathways to Vitality, and analyzes how a congregation might move there from dystrophy, retrogression, or decay.

Appendix 1 contains a simple congregational assessment for vitality using growth and stability factors. Appendix 2 compares resources employed by the various church types. Appendix 3 looks at giving practices in the four church types, while appendix 4 provides a brief comparison of learning and education.

There is one important message to share from vital congregations: Vitality is neither simple nor easy. There is a very good reason why more churches aren't vital: It is hard work. Perhaps the single greatest challenge to vitality is that it requires us to be Christian. We too often confuse being Christian with being nice. We fail to make difficult decisions, challenge inappropriate behaviors, hold people accountable, or establish developmental goals and standards that require real sacrifice and commitment. Making church easy is the opposite of making the church faithful. Vital churches challenge us to remember that the church is God's, not ours, and being Christian disciples is more involved than simply believing in Jesus as the Son of God.

Our world needs what the church, at its best, has to offer: grace, mercy, love, forgiveness, hope, vision, and justice. To love as God loves, to be just, kind, merciful, and grace-filled requires that we become fully alive, fully committed, healthy, and whole. To be the church for the world requires that we become vital.

. . . .

CHAPTER ONE

The Decaying Congregation

I t is difficult to know where to begin when talking about decaying congregations. There are a lot of declining, unstable congregations in The United Methodist Church. Here is a brief list of complaints, concerns, quibbles, and constraints identified by the 363 decaying congregations in this survey and the percentage of churches naming each problem.

Lack of money	97%
Lack of leaders	94%
Lack of commitment	92%
Lack of "new/young" leaders	88%
Burnout/tired	88%
Independent church competition	86%
Too many meetings	84%
Conflict in congregation	82%

Apportionments too high	77%
Building/facility old/costly	71%
No young families	71%
Lack of vision	69%
Newcomers try to change things	62%
Conference doesn't support us	61%
Godless society	56%
Too much change	54%
Getting older	54%

Note that these are the problems cited by the *majority* of congregations surveyed. Talking with leaders from these congregations, one gets the impression that everything is the problem. The morale in these congregations is dismal. The energy level is low, and there is often a sense of hopelessness. Paradoxically, it is clear that the leaders in these congregations love God, love Jesus Christ, and have a deep desire for things to be better. As one pastor related, "I never get up in the morning and say, 'Today I'm going to try to be really ineffective.' Everyone here is trying to be faithful, to do good. It breaks my heart that we work so hard, and see so little to show for it." Sadly, many people in decaying congregations find church to be a trial and a burden, with too few people trying to prop up a ministry in danger of collapse.

"I don't know how it got this way," a lifelong Methodist lay leader told me. "In the 1950s we were *the* church. Everybody who was anybody was here. We had the biggest Sunday school, three worship services, and three full-time pastors. Our parking lot was always full. Our kids got older and moved away, we lost teachers, we went to two services, then one, then we overspent our endowments, and now we look at the future and there isn't one. It all got away from us." Once again, this is not an isolated lament. Many once active, thriving congregations find themselves wondering about tomorrow.

Decaying congregations often follow a common downward spiral. In their infancy, these churches were central to the community where they are located. During the boom years, it was assumed that the success was due mainly to the quality of the program and ministry, and that it would continue to thrive indefinitely. However, as the community demographics shifted, so shifted the fortunes of the congregation. Younger generations departed the area, suburban members relocated to newly emerging congregations, younger families with less disposable income provided less financial support, existing membership aged, as did the physical plant. Before long, the success of the congregation was limited by the strong forces of location and convenience. Congregations lacking a compelling vision and a clear sense of identity and purpose found themselves on the margins, losing ground at an alarming pace. Most hit a level of struggle—the faithful remnant giving all their time, energy, and resources to keep the doors open, the pastor paid, and the insurance policy from expiring—or passed below it, closing their doors.

The daily reality in a decaying congregation is conflicted, confusing, and often contradictory. People want things to be better, but don't want to change. People want newcomers, but fear strangers. People want children, but no disruption or noise. People want the future to look more like the 1950s. In fact, people in decaying congregations don't really seem to know what they want; they just know they aren't content with what they've got.

Sense of Identity

Of all the stability criteria, a strong sense of identity—who we are as a congregation of God's people—is perhaps the most important. "Who are we?" rests at the heart of our entire walk of faith. Individually, we wrestle with this question on a regular basis, but it is every bit as important that we wrestle with it corporately as well.

Decaying congregations tend not to have a strong sense of identity; or they hold a sense of their identity from a bygone day—who they used to be, rather than who they are. In some cases, decaying congregations confuse who they think they *should* be with who they are. With rare exceptions, denominational identity is of little importance. Outside of the congregation, the church has limited or no reputation. Where there is a community identity, it tends not to be around a mission or ministry, but a church supper, bazaar, craft fair, or fellowship event.

When you ask a decaying congregation to describe itself, you almost always hear, "We're a friendly church." Friendliness seems to be a high value with struggling congregations, though in many cases visitors report that these churches are cold, impersonal, exclusionary, and that they were virtually ignored. Decaying congregations are especially drawn to programs that teach welcome and hospitality, though they struggle to implement them.[1]

When asked to describe the congregation, leaders in decaying congregations most commonly listed programs—what the church does, rather than what it believes. For most leaders in this category, the church is a *place* where worship, Sunday school, and fellowship occur. For the majority of congregants (those who attend worship on Sunday morning[2]) the church is quite simply where they go to worship—it serves no larger function and its identity is a given. As one charming gentleman asked me, "Is this a trick question? What do you mean by 'identity'? It's a church—a church is a church—that's what it is." For the majority of people in decaying congregations, this definition suffices.

Shared Clarity of Purpose

If identity asks, *"Who* are we?" then purpose asks, *"Why* are we?" Once again, the question of why the church exists is confusing to many within the decaying congregation. "Christians need a church to go to," responds one retired teacher. "The reason for church is church." This tautology rings true for many congregants and leaders in declining and unstable churches, and may indicate *why* they struggle. In the majority of decaying congregations, the local church is an end in itself, and not a means to a greater end. Most people in decaying churches feel that the church exists for their benefit. It is rare outside of the circles of leadership in unstable congregations to find people who see themselves as ministers, leaders, or active disciples. Attending worship is the baseline criteria for faithfulness. Many members of declining churches talk about what a personal sacrifice it is to fit church into their busy schedules. Church is a convenience, an option among many, and not of central importance to their faith.

For many members of decaying congregations, the purpose of the church is

---

1. Two hundred seventy-eight of the 363 of decaying congregations (77%) participated in some form of Igniting Ministries training. This was one of the most frequently named resources used by decaying congregations, along with books by Bill Easum, Ken Callahan, Rick Warren, Tom Bandy, and the DISCIPLE Bible studies.

2. Worship occurs on Sunday morning in most decaying congregations: 331 of 363 (91%) offer worship experiences only on Sunday before noon. Twenty-nine (8%) offer a Saturday evening option, eleven (3%) offer a Wednesday or Sunday night service, and one offers a Friday night contemplative service.

to give comfort, encouragement, and support. It exists to serve their needs—a place they will be prayed for; visited when sick; and offered services of baptism, marriage, and burial rites. There is a strong consumeristic bent to these congregants view of church.

For those in leadership, the purpose of the church tends to be vague and amorphous. Ask any dozen church leaders, "What is the purpose of the church?" and you receive twelve answers, like, "a place to worship God," "a place to be with other Christians," "to teach people about Jesus," "a place to pray," "to serve the lost, the least, and the last," or "to make disciples of Jesus Christ." Pressed for a fuller explanation of how the congregation lives out the purpose, most church leaders are at a loss for examples. In some cases, leaders can point to one or two people who actively pursue a sense of mission and purpose, but they strive in isolation. In decaying congregations there is a definite lack of shared clarity of purpose.

Focus of the Congregation

There is a basic, simple difference in the orientation of stable and unstable congregations: Stable congregations balance an inward and outward focus; unstable congregations focus inward. Unstable congregations tend to focus on their own needs, their own desires, and their own future. The existing congregation, and particularly the decision-making leaders, dictates what programs to support, what money to spend, what improvements to make, which are generally designed to increase the comfort and enjoyment of the current membership. Money is poured into the building and grounds, and ministries are designed that bring people to the church, rather than sending church members out into the community. In decaying congregations, it is all about "us."

A pastor in Florida offered a helpful distinction to the focus issue between stable and unstable churches. She remarked that it isn't about focusing on "us" rather than "them," but about how we define "us." When we expand our sense of who defines "us" to include all God's people, we tend to be more thoughtful about those beyond the existing congregation. The walls of a local church can become barriers, dividing those who "belong" from those who don't. "Membership has its privileges," the old American Express ads proclaimed. Decaying congregations live by this credo. With limited resources, low morale, and declining support, it is difficult to be expansive. This often results in a "circling the wagons" mentality. Decaying congregations feel that if they don't care for themselves, no one else will. This reflects a pervasive attitude of victimization in declining churches. Many leaders in declining and unstable churches feel as if all kinds of bad things are happening to them, and that they have little or no control over their own destinies. This leads to a highly provincial orientation. It is a challenge to focus on meeting the needs of others when you feel your own needs are not being met.

Another limitation of declining churches is that, while they claim to want new members, they only truly want people who are just like them. One of the most common sources of conflict in declining and unstable churches is related to newcomers. Each new person brings a different perspective, different experiences, and different expectations. As newcomers attempt to become involved—especially in the decision-making processes of the congregation—they cause disruption and call for change. Change is highly threatening in decaying congregations. It inspires fear that the few remaining comforts and familiarities might be lost. Resistance to change is highest in decaying churches.

Awareness and Understanding of God's Vision for the Church

Almost no one in a decaying church argues with the idea that God has a vision and plan for the church. However, members and leaders in decaying congregations tend to deal with the issue abstractly—what God wants and what we want have little to do with each other. One telling difference between stable and unstable congregations is the amount of time leaders spend in prayer and study together. Of the 120 stable congregations in the study, ninety-five (79%) answered "frequently" to the question, "How often do you pray *together* to discern God's will?" Of the 243 unstable congregations, 158 (65%) responded, "rarely/never" to the same question.[3]

Many of the decaying congregations in the study developed a "vision statement," having gone through a wide variety of visioning processes. Paradoxically, congregational leaders who spent the most time developing their statements had the greatest difficulty remembering them. Many churches had their statement framed on a wall or printed weekly in the bulletin, but few

---

3. Note the "together" in the question. The majority of congregational leaders report that they regularly pray for God's guidance in their personal devotional time.

members could quote them. Essentially, the lack of vision is grounded in a basic misunderstanding about the nature of vision. Many congregations approach the "development" of a vision as a program activity; they create a "vision team," and hand off the visioning work as a task. Vision isn't some thing we create; it is something discovered. Vision emerges through discernment as a body of people (in the case of the church, a community of believers) shares their deepest desires, their core values and beliefs, and seek faithful ways to put their gifts to work. A vision isn't mere words you can put on paper. Vision is fluid, always shifting, growing, and changing. Real vision is "written" in people's hearts. The healthiest congregations know their vision deep down. They can call it to mind because it is never far from them. The vision of the people reflects the heart of the people for God. Vision is a struggle in decaying congregations. Whenever a group approaches vision as a task, it is likely missing the point.

Governing and Guiding Values

Values are not behaviors, but the underlying beliefs, opinions, and attitudes upon which behavior is based. We act the way we do because of what we believe in our heart of hearts to be true. Individuals often develop unspoken codes of conduct based on values. In community, values blend and clash, and over time what is truly important is revealed.

In every individual and group there is also a "values gap," a space between what we say we believe (our articulated values) and what we do (our lived values). In the church, we often say that we "love everyone unconditionally." But when someone is significantly different, we find that our love and acceptance has limits. In survey after survey, United Methodists claim to be guided by values of acceptance, justice, generosity, and compassion, but the governing values of our *behaviors* are comfort, security, and the preservation of the familiar.[4]

Decaying congregations rarely, if ever, discuss values. Unstable congregations operate under the false assumption that because we are all Christians, it fol-

---

4. The "lived" values of comfort, safety/security, and preserving the familiar are common values, not only in the church but throughout North American culture. These values hold true across most racial, ethnic, economic, and educational spectra. Most Christians believe in the goodness of mercy, justice, generosity, and compassion, but in actual practice, each of these values can be deeply threatening and uncomfortable. It is one reason why decaying congregations have so much trouble accepting newcomers; newcomers make us uncomfortable, feel insecure, and they threaten the status quo.

lows that we share a common set of values. This is not true. Those who serve in leadership in the congregation tend to have a more expansive view of the church, a deeper knowledge of the Bible, more exposure to fundamental theological and Biblical teachings, and therefore a more global perspective. Often, leaders in the church organize the ministries around a sense of serving a larger community than just the membership of the local church. However, the majority of the membership—especially in decaying congregations—believes that the church exists to serve them. Conflict often arises. The root of such conflict rests in a clash of values, disagreement about purpose, and contradictory visions for the church.

Decision makers in congregations are guided by a desire to strengthen and grow the church. They seek new members, new programs, and new initiatives—often promoting outreach. All of these decisions threaten the status quo.

When the participants in a congregation do not clearly understand the guiding values upon which congregational leaders make their decisions, conflict is almost inevitable. When the values of the congregation are not fully integrated into the sense of identity and purpose, misunderstandings are frequent. When leaders adopt an outward focus of witness and service, while the majority of members hold an inward focus of nurture and care, problems result. This is the ongoing reality of a majority of decaying congregations. A whopping 91% of the decaying churches report some form of destructive conflict, generally grounded in disagreement over the "appropriate" ministry of the church. Where unresolved conflict is present, it is generally symptomatic of a clash of core values.

Most decaying congregations have no clear process for dealing with conflict and disagreement. Communication tends to be a weakness in most unstable congregations, and often disagreeable tasks of conflict resolution or peace keeping fall to the pastor-in-charge. This can be devastating to a local church, especially smaller churches. It is very difficult for the pastor to mediate a conflict without appearing to take sides. Once a pastoral leader is perceived to be on one side or the other, his or her effectiveness as a pastor to the whole congregation is essentially over. Stable congregations tend to have a proactive approach to conflict. They address it openly, honestly, and with appropriate mediation from a non-involved third party. Unstable congregations are more reactive, unwisely assuming that good, decent Christian people can work things out themselves. The ability to deal with conflict, name and confront inappropriate behavior[5],

5. Another critical difference between unstable and stable congregations is the presence of what I call "toxic influencers." In both decaying and dystrophic congregations, there are individuals who work behind the scenes to "poison" people's minds against new ideas, changes,

and gracefully forgive and move on is one of the critical hurdles to make the shift from instability to stability.

Impact Awareness

Nothing was more surprising, or significant than this concept of "impact awareness." Impact awareness simply means knowing the value that results from the ministries, programs, and experiences of the local church. How are people's lives changed by worship? What changes in people's attitudes and actions when they study the Bible or pray together? Where do people live their faith? In what ways do people become more Christlike? How is a person living, thinking, and behaving differently today than when they joined the community of faith? Vital churches can answer each of these questions. Decaying churches cannot.

When asked the question, "As you design worship in this congregation, what expectations do you have about what people will experience?" the vast majority of decaying church leaders asked, "What do you mean?" The idea that the worship experience should be designed to help people experience the presence of God was foreign to most of the leaders in unstable congregations. As one pastor with forty-one years in the ministry said, "It's our job to lead a service, what happens to the congregation is between them and God."

However, to another pastor, this concept stirred some deep feeling and helped her articulate a problem she experiences in the church she is serving. "We are a 'flat-line' church. There is no upward spiral, no ongoing development. Here, Christian is a state of being. You either are one or you're not. There is no sense of journey. When you asked your question, I thought, 'That's stupid. We do what we do because we're the church—it's what churches do.' But as we talked about it I realized, I haven't the foggiest idea what happens to people after they worship here. For all I know it goes in one ear and out the other. It

---

(especially to worship services), innovations, and new people in leadership. These people hold incredible power to undermine the authority of elected leaders and working groups. They often hold the church hostage through threat of leaving or withholding money. More remarkably, they are allowed to function this way, often for years, and their behavior is never exposed to the light of day and dealt with. Vital and retrogressive congregations simply refuse to allow such behavior to continue, even to the point of actually asking these toxic influencers to leave the congregation.

shouldn't be that way. Day-by-day, week-by-week, people should be growing more and more into the image of Christ. We [the congregation's leaders] need to know how we are helping—or not helping—that to happen."

Impact awareness happens only by design. Most congregations do not do it naturally. First, worship leaders, small group leaders, Sunday school and Bible study teachers need to design experiences with clear objectives. If we want to explore the grace of God, for example, we want to make sure that participants come away with a working knowledge and understanding of prevenient, justifying, sanctifying grace in the Wesleyan tradition, and its relationship to Wesley's teachings about Christian perfection. Second, these leaders need some way to measure and assess how well these objectives are met, how well people learn what is of central importance. Last, leaders need some way to evaluate impact, to answer the question, "So what?" What difference does what we learn and experience make on the way we live our lives? How is our growing faith made manifest in our thoughts, words, and actions? Not one of the decaying congregations had a clear process for evaluating the impact of their ministries on participating members.

Leadership in the Congregation

In most decaying churches, a small segment of members provide a representative leadership for the whole congregation. One individual may assume as many as seven or eight different leadership responsibilities. Recruiting new leaders is often a problem, and rarely is there an integrated plan for leadership development, training, and support. Members of the Committee on Lay Leadership use terms like "filling slots," "cornering people," and "finding people who can't say no," when describing the nomination process for electing leaders at charge conference. In many decaying congregations a reliance on "Time, Talent, and Treasure" surveys, or an abridged and aborted spiritual gifts discovery process exists. Preexisting committees and pre-determined tasks create a demand for warm bodies to assume responsibility. Rarely, if ever, do decaying congregations align work with true gifts, passions, or a sense of calling. In fact, many leaders report that the work they do for the church has very little to do with what they believe God has gifted and called them to. Their support of the work of the church is done from a sense of responsibility and a desire to do what is needed.

There is a deep sense of pain in leaders of decaying congregations. For a host of reasons, people make heart-felt, lasting commitments to their congregation. They want it to thrive. They want to see it strong, but they lack the knowledge and experience to strengthen it. Leaders in decaying congregations are constantly on the lookout for resources that might solve their problems. Too often, this results in a "magic bullet" approach, the belief that there is a simple, clear, easy remedy to current ills. This deep desire explains the popularity of so many church resources. Only in very rare situations can the answers appropriate to one setting be of lasting help when applied to another context. The majority of leaders in decaying congregations have completely bought into the cultural definitions of "successful" churches—big buildings, big programs, big parking lots, long-term pastorates, and big budgets. The leaders of decaying congregations spend a disproportionate amount of time looking externally for answers to their problems, rather than gaining insight into their own unique context. Not one of the vital congregations found health by borrowing ideas from other churches, no matter how "successful" the other churches might be.

One significant difference between leadership in stable and unstable congregations rests in how time is used when leaders gather. Stable congregations devote a large amount of time to learning, strategic thinking, and the practice of spiritual disciplines. Unstable congregations report being "too busy" to "waste time" in these pursuits. Instead, time is given to reflecting on the past, on problems, and dealing with day-to-day decisions. In stable congregations, there are clearly differentiated leadership roles—*visioning, futuring,* and *management*[6]—while in unstable congregations the same people have responsibility for all three aspects. Because the short-term demands of management are ubiquitous, they usually overshadow long-term needs. This leads to a shortsighted, reactive style of leadership prevalent in decaying congregations.

The difficulties experienced by leaders in decaying churches are interwoven with the lack of a sense of identity, purpose, and vision, all of which leads to an inward focus. It is very difficult to determine the appropriate kinds of

---

6. The *visioning* function of leadership looks at the big picture, focusing on where God is leading the congregation in the future. This is the work of setting priorities and goals for the congregation. *Futuring* is the work of creating the structures and processes necessary to move the congregation into the future. This requires knowledge of both the goals and objectives for the future as well as the resources and knowledge in the present. Futuring helps create what doesn't already exist so the church can do new and appropriate things in the future. The *management* function attends to the day-to-day decisions and needs of the congregation. It maximizes the congregation's effectiveness in the short-term, and pays little or no attention to the long-term goals of the church.

leadership that are needed unless there is a clear understanding of where you want to go. As one older laywoman commented, "It feels like we've been walking in circles for a long time. We know we're in the right vicinity, but we just don't know where to go next." This sense of "going through the motions" is common in decaying congregations.

The Role of the Appointed Pastor(s)

Nowhere is there greater frustration expressed by clergy than in decaying congregations. Full-time pastors in these churches work an average of sixty-eight and a half hours per week. They attend most meetings in the church; have primary responsibility for leading worship and preaching, visitation and counseling, responding to questions throughout the week; serve as intermediary to the community where the church is located; and assume teaching duties, attend fellowship events, and organize activities. Forty percent of the pastors participating in this study lead a youth group, and 89% teach confirmation. Most serve as "tenth trustees," interpreting *The Book of Discipline* and legal codes for the church. Three quarters (77%) report that the majority of their church members expect them to perform all of these functions as a normal part of the job. Low morale, physical and emotional problems, stress, family turmoil, and burnout are common concerns among the pastors of decaying congregations.

There are five key factors contributing to the untenable position of pastors in decaying churches: ineffective Pastor-Parish Relations Committees (or Staff-Parish Relations Committee, in some cases), unwillingness to stand up for self and family, poor self-care, inability to delegate responsibility, and an unclear sense of call.

In The United Methodist Church system, a safeguard against unrealistic expectation and demands exists in the form of the Pastor-Parish Relations Committee (PPRC). A critical role of this committee is to work with the appointed leaders to set priorities, determine the best use of the pastor's time, and to make recommendations to the Church Council concerning ways to address ministry needs that are not a high priority for the pastor. The PPRC serves to protect the pastoral leader, while making sure that the congregation's needs are being met. The PPRC reminds the church that a pastor is only one person, and can only do so much—that this person is uniquely gifted, and the congregation can be best served by helping to free the pastor for the work in which he or she excels. This does not work well in decaying congregations. The vast majority (86%) of PPRC chairs and members confess to being unclear about the work of their committee. Very few understand their role as collaborative supervision, counsel, and liaison between clergy and congregation. When this level of support, supervision, and interpretation is absent, those who bear the brunt of the loss are the clergy leaders and their families.

Of the pastoral leadership in the four different church types, those least likely to defend themselves and their families are the pastors of decaying congregations. "My call is to the church, to be a servant, and I have no right to put my needs before the Lord's," commented one soon-to-be-retired pastor. "But I have paid a heavy, heavy cost," he continued. Married and divorced twice, estranged from his daughter and grandchildren, suffering high-blood pressure and surviving two heart attacks, this poor man illustrates the confusion between servant leadership and slavery. Many pastors in similar situations claim that they have no choice in the matter: The church comes first. While a noble sentiment at one level, the implications are staggering. Certainly sacrifices must be made, but the implicit message sent by these men and women is that "abundant life in Christ," leads to ill health, broken relationships, hopelessness, despair, and resentment. This is not a compelling image of the life and walk of a Christian disciple, especially when so many others make the journey full of joy, energy, conviction, hope, and purpose. Healthy leaders know their limitations; set boundaries, discipline themselves, communicate these limits and boundaries to others, and protect themselves so that they might stay effective for the long term.

Healthy leaders also know that they must renew themselves in body, mind, and spirit. Regular exercise, good diet, a program for learning, and spiritual discipline are sorely lacking in the lives of two-thirds (66%) of the pastors of decaying congregations. The most common reason given for this lack is "not enough time." As the demands of the job expand, they displace personal time. Many of the pastors in this category lament that they only pray, read Scripture, or worship "professionally"; that is, when they perform these functions as a part of their leadership role. Four out of five pastors surveyed report that they "regularly" give up their day off for work related reasons. Twenty-one percent report that they have not taken a vacation in the past three years.[7] The pastors serving decaying congregations are more prone to debilitating health problems than leaders of any other church type. The stresses and strains of leading struggling congregations exact an enormous toll.

---

7. As opposed to 4% of pastors in dystrophic congregations and less than 1% in both retrogressive and vital congregations.

Another contributing factor is the inability or unwillingness of pastors in decaying congregations to delegate responsibility, share authority, and entrust leadership to the laity. Most pastoral leaders complain that laity are unwilling to assume leadership. In some cases this is true, but often members of the congregation perceive these pastors as autocratic, micro-managers who prefer to work alone. When pressed, four out of five pastoral leaders confess that they were never taught management and supervision skills in college or seminary. As the demands of a congregation grow, the pastor's ability to "do everything" diminishes.

One thirty-year clergy leader explained part of the problem this way, "I started fresh from seminary in a church of about fifty members. I could handle everything without breaking a sweat. I got "bumped up" to a church of about 120 members—still very manageable on my own. When I took a third appointment of over 250 members, things started to get tough. People complained that I let things fall through the cracks. The church grew to over 400 members and I about had a nervous breakdown. I got ulcers, lost hair, lost sleep, got cranky, and finally asked (my district superintendent) to move me. I had the same problems in my next church, and the next, never staying for more than a couple years any one place. When I finally got appointed to another one-hundred-member church, I was fine. I loved it, they loved me, a match made in heaven. Now I realize that I was my own worst enemy. If I only knew then what I know now." This is not an uncommon story in decaying congregations.

One last significant factor contributing to the distress of pastors in decaying congregations is ambiguity concerning call to ministry. Nine out of ten pastors in unstable, declining churches mourn a lost sense of purpose. The very reason they entered ministry initially fades and disappears when confronted by the demanding reality of running a church. Many pastors poignantly remember moments, experiences, or events representing a prophetic call from God to serve. Few pastoral leaders in decaying congregations report that they are fulfilling their call or living up to the potential they once believed possible. Dozens of pastors share heartbreaking stories of disillusionment and regret.

When call is subsumed by task, the entire church is hurt. For those who believe that they are gifted of God, called to serve, charged to lead, and responsible for the spiritual development in a community of faith, nothing is more demoralizing than squashing petty disputes, chasing pennies, and debating endlessly whether or not to pay apportionments. The sense of call, the understanding of gifts, and the passion to serve and lead shape the identity of the pastoral leader. Once a pastor ceases to lead from her true identity, she ceases to be fully effective, and she battles to feel good about her ministry.

Programmatic Design

The running joke in many churches is that every new idea is met by the classic response: "We've never done it that way before." This is actually true in many decaying churches. Once programs become institutionalized, they become "the church"—one way of worshiping, one roster of Sunday school classes, one way of doing fundraising, evangelism, and outreach.

For the majority of unstable congregations—both decaying and dystrophic—what we do defines who we are. Our activities are our selling points. We invite people to services, classes, programs, and events. Stable congregations appeal more to building relationships grounded in shared values and common aspirations. Decaying congregations confuse means and ends. Many leaders in decaying churches have difficulty explaining why they do the things they do. "We worship because we worship; we have Sunday school because we've always had Sunday school, and we have our Sunday suppers because that's what we do. Nobody here asks, 'Why?' We do it just 'because,'" explained a retired builder of his country church.

In such rigid settings, change is difficult, and evaluation of effectiveness rarely occurs. People find comfort in familiarity, making assumptions about what constitutes "normal." Newcomers and visitors often feel left out—they don't speak the language, share the history, or understand the traditions.

Many wonderful practices exist in our congregations. Our traditions are deeply meaningful and important, but they are never more important than our mission and purpose. The church belongs to God, the ministry is greater than meeting the needs of the existing membership, and those who attend a church are privileged to be "the body of Christ." Programs serve one purpose: to enable people to grow in their discipleship. All that we do in a church works to weave us together, empowering us to be Christ for the world. It is nice to find comfort and security in our home church, but we must not stop there.

Leaders in seven out of ten decaying congregations—both clergy and laity—contend that their church is "stuck." They report that all attempts to alter long-standing services, classes, and programs meet strong resistance. In most of these cases, the changes proposed have not been handled well (another shortcoming in decaying settings). Growing churches, dystrophic as well as vital, possess a solid understanding of change theory and ways to navigate resistance. Many decaying congregations lack deep insight into the nature of change and the problems inherent in breaking from the familiar.

Ultimately, programs serve as building blocks—source material used to fulfill our mission and realize our potential as Christian disciples. When programs exist as isolated experiences, divorced from a larger vision for what it means to be a healthy, thriving church, they become "sacred cows"; preserved not for the value they provide, but simply because we like them.

Organizational Structure

A particularly challenging and difficult observation about decaying congregations is that they are designed to decay. In the vast majority of decaying churches, committees, boards, councils, work areas, and task forces are not designed to achieve particular ends. Instead, they follow a prescribed format (often determined by the forms required to be filed at charge conference) with no regard to their appropriateness for the work. In decaying congregation, function follows form. Groups of people elected to leadership positions struggle to figure out what they need to do. Healthy congregations organize around priorities, analyzing what each one requires to be successfully preformed. In unstable congregations, everything has equal importance—but, when everything is a priority, nothing is a priority.

Form must follow function. How we organize to do our work must be appropriate to the tasks. When our structures and processes limit what we do, we restrict the guidance of the Holy Spirit and become less able to respond to emerging needs. Structures work best when they are designed to meet specific needs and yield specific outcomes.

Only by defining outcomes can we determine not only *how* to achieve them, but *who* we need to achieve them. In decaying congregations, the recruitment and election of leaders tends to be an arbitrary process. Little consideration is given to individual's gifts, passions, interests, or spiritual development. Instead, the primary criteria for selection in decaying churches are:

availability

past willingness to serve

devotion to the congregation

None of these criteria are bad in and of themselves, but they are almost certain to generate poor results if they are the *only* criteria.

There is a great deal of confusion among the leaders of decaying congregations concerning exactly what they have agreed to do. Just over 74% of those surveyed said they received little or no training for their job, little or no explanation of the requirements of their role, and no clear goals or objectives for their work. One result of this ambiguity is a high level of absenteeism at meetings in unstable congregations. The average attendance at meetings in decaying congregations is only 55% of the elected leaders.

Surprisingly, more time is spent devoted to meetings in unstable congregations than in stable congregations.[8] However, leaders of decaying churches complain that most meetings are a waste of time, poorly run, and virtually ineffective. One pastor characterized meetings in her church as "a black hole draining resources, energy, interest, and talent. By the time we finish meeting we're too tired and fed up to do ministry."

Money

Money, or lack of money, is the obsession of many decaying congregations. "There is never enough, and what little we have is already spent. If we could only get our finances in order, we could concentrate on other things," is a common refrain. However, the paradox is that churches most focused on money have the greatest money problems. Churches focusing on spiritual formation, discipleship, and building community in Christ have the fewest financial concerns.

Decaying and dystrophic congregations predominantly associate money with stewardship.[9] Ninety-three percent of unstable congregations hold annual financial commitment/giving campaigns (generally called "stewardship campaigns") as the major way they fund the ministry of the local church.[10]

---

8. Meeting hours per week = number of hours each week scheduled for administrative, programmatic, staff, planning, and budgetary meetings. Decaying: 9.25, Dystrophic: 11.75, Retrogressive: 4.0, Vital: 5.5. Church leaders in unstable congregations spend almost twice as much time in meetings as those in stable congregations.

9. Stewardship is defined more holistically and spiritually in the stable retrogressive and vital congregations. The practices that define stewardship in stable congregations concern the way we behave in our community and world. Dystrophic and decaying congregations define stewardship in terms of the way members behave toward the institutional church.

10. None of the 120 stable churches in this study hold annual giving campaigns/programs. The relationship of retrogressive and vital congregations to money and giving will be discussed in chapters 3 and 4.

Of major concern to most decaying congregations are the connectional funds (apportionments, disciplinary obligations, and ministry shares) they are required to pay. Many view these as a "denominational tax," an unfair burden imposed by the system that places the local church in debt before the year even begins. Very rarely do the leaders in struggling congregations speak with positive regard about apportionments.

Apart from the required funds designated by apportionments, most decaying congregations give very little to missions. Mission giving accounts for approximately 2.3% of the total church budget in decaying congregations. The vast majority of budget (83%) is relegated to pastoral support, insurance, maintenance, staff, overhead, and property. Monies designated for program generally support existing needs. Very little exists to launch new programs or initiatives.

Leaders and members alike find money talk uncomfortable. Pastors claim that people resent stewardship sermons and financial appeals, and some members claim that the church is "only interested in their money." On average, 10–15% of the membership of decaying congregations provides 90% of the financial support. In some cases, one or two giving units (individuals or families) provide an inordinate portion of the congregational income. This leaves the church in a precarious position. Should these "deep-pocket givers" leave, die, or withhold their giving, the financial support of the church could collapse. Dozens of pastors and laity leaders share stories of their churches held hostage by members threatening to withhold their offerings. In extreme cases, those who control the purse strings control the church.

Financial reserves tend to be slim in decaying congregations. Very few of these churches have endowments, investments, or capital reserves. Nor do they have a plan in place to receive gifts, bequests, memorials, or designated funds. Rarely do the leaders of decaying congregations develop funding plans for new, emerging, or cooperative ministries. As with so many other aspects of congregational life, decaying churches adopt a reactive, rather than proactive, approach to money.

Budgeting tends to be expense-side planning only. Decaying congregations gather information on what the ministry will cost in the coming year, project income against expenses, then figure ways to cut costs to stretch income to cover outgo. The other three church types develop a ministry plan, figure out what the various projects will require, and then develop plans to adequately fund them.

One common complaint in decaying congregations is the undue influence held by the church treasurer or financial secretary. In many cases, these officers of the church operate individually and independently, withholding critical information, making decisions about the distribution of funds, and refusing to share records with other leaders of the church. Decaying congregations also tend to be lax in conducting external audits and filing required legal forms and paperwork. A decided lack of professionalism exists in some decaying congregations where money is concerned.

The Role of Worship in the Life of the Congregation

Worship is of central importance to the people of decaying congregations. In fact, a significant number of participants in decaying congregations define attending worship as "going to church," and they have no deeper involvement beyond their one hour on Sunday morning. Sunday morning worship becomes a catchall in these settings. Because this is the only time in the week that the church gathers together, everything must be squeezed into sixty minutes. Worship loses its focus and integrity as it becomes "worship and . . ."— worship and announcements, worship and stewardship, worship and evangelism, worship and missions. The focus on God and the invitation to offer God thanks, praise, and commitment is subsumed by activity and busyness. Many people leave worship feeling exhausted by all the chaos and rush. When sacraments or special observances are added to the mix, services "run long" and some people grow restive and aggravated. It is not uncommon for members of decaying congregations to stay home on communion Sundays. This is just one of many symptoms of the lack of a theology of worship in most decaying churches.

In one-on-one interviews, participants in decaying congregations were least able to answer questions about the elements of worship.[11] I probed to explore the question, "Why do we worship?" In decaying congregations, the prevalent

---

11. I asked a sample in each of the four church types to explain to me why worship contained such practices as "confession and pardon," "affirmations of faith," "offering time," "pastoral prayers," "reading of Scripture," "sermons," "invitation to discipleship," "benediction," etc. Unstable congregational participants tended not to be able to explain why United Methodists worship as they do, nor could they explain the significance of most worship practices.

response is, "because that's what churches do." Participants in decaying congregations enter worship with the lowest expectations.[12] While not true for everyone, for a majority of participants in decaying congregations, worship means going through the motions.

One other question about worship caused deep confusion to members of decaying congregations: "How does the worship experience each week impact your daily life?" The answers, while varied, made very clear that members of the decaying type church view worship as primarily about them, rather than God. Most responded that worship made them feel better, helped calm them, provided strength for the week to come, or provided a break from the world. Twenty-three out of twenty-five respondents (96%) listed personal benefits as the reason they attend worship. This contrasts greatly with stable congregations where the benefits have to do with strengthening relationship with God, more deeply understanding God's will, and deepening the sense of shared identity with a community of faith. Personal benefits are collateral in stable churches, rather than primary.

The Role of Education in the Life of the Congregation

In the vast majority of decaying congregations, Christian education equals Sunday school. In a minority of cases, a few small groups may exist, but they comprise a very small percentage of the total number of participants. And in almost 20% of the congregations (seventy-two of the 363), Sunday school is provided primarily for children and youth. Christian education, and learning in general, tends to be a low priority in most decaying churches.

When pushed to explain the importance of Christian education in decaying churches, responses fell into three general categories: 1) we have always had Sunday school and/or Bible studies in the past, therefore we need to have them now; 2) children need to be taught the Bible and how to live good Christian lives; and, 3) we need Sunday school classes and/or Bible studies to draw new members to the church. With the exception of a few individuals, no real vision

12. The question was posed, "What do you expect to happen when you worship God?" The respondents from the decaying sample had the most trouble understanding the question, and confessed that they most often had no expectations. Almost 50% responded that they came to church on Sunday to be with friends and acquaintances.

for an ongoing course of spiritual development and learning appeared in any of the decaying congregations.

The understanding of the need for, and value of, Christian education illuminates one of the more interesting problems prevalent in decaying churches: compartmentalization. The respondents from decaying congregations experienced the greatest difficulty in explaining how their church life and their home and work life interacted. As one gentlemen explained, "Going to church helps me be a better person. But, quite frankly, I don't think much about it through the week." This is not an uncommon sentiment in decaying congregations. With the exception of the most deeply involved (approximately 10–15%) the vast majority of participants "fit church in" to their lives. I polled hundreds of people from decaying churches as they left Bible studies and Sunday school classes, asking what impact their experience would have on their lives once they returned home. The most common response was, "Um, what do you mean?" followed by "none" and "not much." Many people told me they thought it was a silly question.[13]

One significant aspect of the decaying church worldview seems to be that Christian education and learning is for children. The concept of lifelong learning has limited currency in decaying settings. Almost no decaying churches possessed anything remotely related to a comprehensive learning plan for Christian disciples. Growth and development standards were absent as well. Most adults in these settings feel that they are fully formed, and that their confession of Christ as Savior and Lord is all that is required. This reinforces the sense of purpose, identity, and focus in decaying congregations—turned inward, very personal and private, and lacking an "action" component. One woman told me, "I haven't missed church or Sunday school in over fifteen years. That's got to be worth a few stars in my crown." This same woman was unable to tell me how her involvement these fifteen years have changed her or helped her become more Christlike.

A key problem of education in decaying congregations is that it doesn't connect to anything. Class offering are a hodge-podge of curriculum-of-the-month, latest Christian bestseller, current topical theme, etc. Sitting with teachers, Sunday school superintendents, and Christian education chairpersons provided one more insight into unstable churches—they lack standards for

13. However, in all three other church types, people were able to give me thoughtful, substantive answers.

evaluating progress. I provided a simple single-page survey to Christian education leaders in all four of the church types that asked, "What should people have learned/know by the time they are . . . " (four years old? ten years old? fifteen years old? twenty? thirty? forty? fifty? sixty? seventy? eighty?) The answers given by leaders of decaying congregations were very simple, vague, and incomplete.[14] Without judging the criteria generated by the leaders in decaying congregations, I asked them how they determined their effectiveness in reaching these goals. Only a few (seventeen of 363) had any plan or process for evaluating how effectively people were learning these key lessons. Even fewer used any kind of criteria to determine what curriculum to use in their various classes. One woman summed it up nicely when she said, "We buy materials from Cokesbury and David C. Cook. We just assume you all know what you're doing and that we can trust your stuff. We figure that if a child goes through seven or eight years of Sunday school, they will learn everything they need to."

Whereas worship attendance in most decaying congregations averages around one-third of the total membership, Sunday school attendance generally averages less than 20%, and most people who attend Bible studies or special learning groups through the week are the same people in Sunday school or in the inner circle of congregational leadership. Christian education, therefore, is not a high priority of decaying congregations, though a small segment of the congregation may be deeply devoted to it.

The Congregation's Relationship to the Community

Every local church exists in a unique community setting. One growing concern in United Methodism is that many of our churches no longer reflect the community in which they are located. As members move from the city to the suburbs and beyond, the majority of participants in a congregation may drive five miles or

---

14. Responses by vital and retrogressive congregations were highly detailed, often requiring extra pages to complete, and containing specific answers to every age group. Responses by decaying and dystrophic congregations were general, short, and most lumped together all the adult levels. By consensus, decaying congregations believe that a four-year-old should know that Jesus loves them and that Jesus is God's Son. By age ten, a child should know the difference between good and bad, and should know that Christians try to do good and avoid bad. By fifteen, teenagers should know that Jesus died for their sins and that by doing what Jesus says you can go to heaven. By twenty and beyond, adults should know that it is important to pray, read the Bible, and go to church, and to try to live a clean and honest life.

more to get to their church. Fewer and fewer people walk to church. In the case of urban and inner city congregations, most of the people living within walking distance are of a minority race, ethnicity, economic situation, or educational level from the existing congregation. This is especially true for decaying churches. Decaying churches struggle mightily with the tensions caused by shifting demographic and ethnographic realities. I visited many churches with fencing, razor wire, iron bars over windows, multiple security locks and deadbolts, and electronic security systems. In many communities, there is a very strong us/them message being sent. Many congregational leaders feel hopelessly victimized by their location and setting. Many are ill equipped to deal with the changing realities.

One of the common experiences I enjoyed throughout this study was visiting hundreds of towns, cities, suburbs, and rural communities where I either walked around or drove, asking people I met, "What can you tell me about XYZ United Methodist Church?" This simple question told me a lot about the church's relationship to its community. In the case of decaying congregations, two responses were common. First, most people in the community couldn't tell me anything about the church, unsure even of its location. The second response was to tell me about some activity associated with the church: "Oh, they do the chicken and biscuit supper," "You mean, the church that has the strawberry festival," or "My sister's kid goes to daycare there." Seldom were people able to tell me anything about the church's witness or mission. Not once did I hear someone tell me about the powerful social witness or that the church was renowned for its spirituality and focus on God.[15] I was alarmed by the number of times I was within two city blocks of a church, and merchants, residents, and community leaders were unaware of the church I was talking about.

It is easy to blame people for not knowing about their community, but in the case of building a relationship between the church and surrounding community, responsibility falls to the church. When churches get outside of themselves and take the mission and ministry into the world, people know about it. Too many of our congregations operate from a "fortress/survival" mentality. It is "us" against "them." Many members feel that the world is unsafe, unkind, unrelenting, so the church needs to become a port in the storm, a saving station, a sanctuary, if you will, but this is only one aspect of a church's role and function. Certainly, the church offers comfort, support, and shelter, but we are the

---

15. I did hear both of these things about many retrogressive and vital congregations, and about a handful of dystrophic churches.

church; those who are so blessed have an obligation to extend the blessing. Decaying congregations seem to have forgotten the second part.

Of the four church types, decaying congregations tend to network the least with other churches and agencies in the community. Many decaying churches try to do everything themselves. They are the least ecumenical, the least collaborative, and the least involved in community service. It is no surprise, then, that decaying congregations make the smallest positive impact on their communities.

One sad result of this is that decaying churches often focus on the wrong things. Many of our decaying congregations have been bombarded by the "bigger is better" message of so many church growth resources. Leaders in these congregations attend leadership academies, workshops, and church development seminars, seeking the magic formula that will transform them from a small church frog into a megachurch prince. They waste precious resources attempting to learn to become something they aren't. Most decaying congregations are not in ideal situations. No matter how well they emulate the premiere teaching churches, they will not grow. In fact, they may not even survive. For a whole host of reasons, numeric growth is beyond their reach. However, while they may not be able to attract more people to come to them, they are strategically located to reach out to many more people than they actually do. One of the fundamental shifts that vital and retrogressive congregations make is that they stop counting the number of people who come to them, and they count instead the number of people served or the number of lives touched by participants in the congregation. This is a huge, significant shift. Unstable congregations count inputs (the number of members, the number of worship attendees, the number of dollars donated). Stable congregations count outputs (number of people helped, reached, loved, and served). One of the distinguishing marks between stable and unstable churches is the way they evaluate effectiveness. When the focus is on outputs, the whole community knows what you do. When it is on inputs, only you know what you do, and even that is questionable.

The Congregation's Relationship to the Connectional System

Here things get tricky. The measure often used to judge support of the connectional system is how well, how faithfully a congregation pays their apportionments (Conference and World Service funds). This is an inadequate measure, however, because some of our most congregational (anti-connectional) churches pay their apportionments in full each year, and many churches that hold the conference and denomination in high regard pay virtually nothing. What does quickly emerge from conversation with the leaders of decaying congregations is a deep ambivalence about the connection.

For the most part, decaying congregations are not deeply invested in the "United Methodist" denominational identity.[16] Larger churches boast of gaining the clout necessary to call their own shots, hold onto the pastor they want, and behave in classically congregational ways. Very few of the leaders I spoke with had much knowledge of Methodist history, Wesleyan teachings, or denominational doctrine and polity.

Many decaying congregations feel they have been badly treated by the connectional system. Some report that every time they get a good pastor, he or she is taken away from them after a couple years. Others lament that the only attention they received from the conference is when they fail to pay apportionments. Still others feel that the conference is indifferent to their plight; that the conference could care less whether the church survived or closed. Many express a deep resentment that the conference has the power to tell them what to do, without a commensurate responsibility to listen to their needs.

Some of these complaints are valid, and they point out that our Annual Conference system is less than perfect. However, it also illustrates a common problem endemic to decaying churches—the attitude that, "it's not our fault." Decaying congregations have 1,001 explanations for why they are struggling, but very few of them point to themselves. "The conference doesn't support us," "the conference taxes us," "there's too much competition," "new people won't step up," and on and on. In most cases where decaying congregations have poor relationships with the Annual Conference, the leaders use the conference as a scapegoat for their problems. All of the other three church types made a monumental

---

16. This is actually true of the entire denomination. For almost forty years, The United Methodist Church has come to depend on transfers from other faith communions for its expansion and growth. Fewer members join by profession of faith and through confirmation. As more "lapsed" Baptists, Presbyterians, Lutherans, Episcopalians, Roman Catholics, etc., join the ranks of United Methodism, the less tied we are to our Wesleyan roots. Since decaying and dystrophic congregations tend to do a very poor job orienting new members to The United Methodist theology, tradition, and polity, newer participants view their new congregation through their old church filters. More and more United Methodists question the connectional system, itinerancy, apportionments, the episcopacy and district superintendency, etc., because they come from such different backgrounds.

decision at some point: "Nobody else will do this for us. We have to take responsibility for ourselves."

Many leaders in decaying congregations do not like hearing this. Some of their complaints are legitimate, and often they do not receive the kind of help that would benefit them most. However, the problems the conference can solve are usually symptomatic, not root causes. Here things come full circle. When a congregation is unclear about its identity, including its denominational heritage, doctrine, polity, and theology, it has little clarity about what it needs to be effective. If a congregation lacks a deep understanding of its mission, vision, values, and reason for existence, it cannot work within the connectional system to match need with pastoral gifts and skills. Without an integrated focus (the rich blend of inward development and outward service) it limits the ways it can connect with the larger system.

The connectional system is currently out of order. It's broken. Congregations should not have the option to decide whether they will or won't be connectional. United Methodist Churches, by definition, are connectional, warts and all. The fact that so many growing churches get to play by their own set of rules, that so many pastors operate as "lone ranger" free agents, and that so many congregations resist and resent the system, indicates that nobody's really clear anymore about what's important. There is some truth to the fact that many churches never hear from the conference except around apportionments, but so what? Doctors don't tend to call patients to remind them to make appointments. The patient has to take responsibility for his or her own health and wellbeing. The benefits afforded by our connectional system are many, but they only accrue to the extent that we invest in them. Decaying congregations are in a reactive relationship to the Annual Conference. Healthier churches are proactive and they work collaboratively within the system to bring forth the greatest benefits.

Summarizing the Decaying Condition

No church wants to decay. No church leader ever sets out to do a poor job. Many fine, deeply committed, wonderfully Christlike men and women strive courageously to do good work for God's glory. It is doubly tragic for these fine folks that they work so hard and see so little in return. It is not a matter of intent, energy, commitment, or dedication. It is, to use a cliché, a matter of working smarter, not harder.

Few decaying congregations are positioned, physically or metaphorically, for growth. However, with the exception of one or two churches in such deep trouble that nothing much will help, all decaying congregations can work on their sustainability. Though it is challenging work, requiring a good amount of time and energy, almost any decaying church can begin to rebuild a sound foundation by attending to the questions of identity, purpose, focus, discernment of God's vision, and core values. Almost every stable congregation moved toward stability and sustainability by setting one or two compelling, comprehensive goals and aligning all their energy, effort, and resources to achieving those ends.

Decaying congregations need to shake free themselves from the "bigger is better" mentality of the megachurch fad. Bigger is simply bigger, not necessarily better. Annual Conference leaders can offer the "gospel" message to smaller, struggling churches that size isn't everything, integrity is. Being great at one thing is better stewardship than being mediocre at a lot of things. Reaching out as the hands and voice of Christ is more important than gathering in to set new attendance marks. The challenge for all our churches is to be better, not just bigger; to be faithful to fulfill our mission, God's vision, and our purpose. Our world doesn't need more church members. What the world needs is authentic disciples, living in true community, who become the body of Christ for the world. I visited many churches that may never again grow numerically, but had almost unlimited potential to serve their community and world, nonetheless.

Decay is as much a state of mind as it is a physical reality. Once our membership begins to age and numbers decrease, we begin to despair. Fewer younger members means fewer children. Fewer bodies in attendance means fewer dollars in the plate. The downward spiral begins. People begin to wish for days gone by—times when the Sunday school was full to overflowing and ushers had to set up extra chairs in the aisles on Christmas Eve and Easter. Attention drifts to the past, and no one has eyes for the future. All this happens to a congregation because it forgets who it is and why it exists. The solution is simple, but not easy. Decaying congregations need to get back to the basics—to start over with the "who," "what," and "why" questions—or they will needlessly suffer their own demise.

CHAPTER TWO

● ● ● ● ● ● ● ● ● ● ● ● ● ● ● ● ● ●

The Dystrophic Congregation

At the outset, I want to be very clear: I am not saying that *big* is *bad*. There are big churches, fast growing churches, that express many forms of vitality. They touch many lives, do much good, make a big difference, but for all this, they are very fragile and unsustainable over a long period. Looking at the ten largest churches in our denomination when the Methodist Church merged with the Evangelical United Brethren in 1968, you will note that none of them maintained their status. In fact, they all find themselves today in the decaying quadrant. Dystrophic congregations may look quite healthy today, but because they have not learned the lessons of history, they are doomed to repeat them.

Thirty-two percent (234 out of 717) of the congregations in the study are both growing and unsustainable over time. Seven of the churches report over 5,000 members, eleven additional churches boast over 3,000 members, while thirty-five more congregations have more than 1,000 members on their books. The two largest segments of dystrophic churches were 750+ members (60 churches) and 500+ members (76). Smaller congregations fall into the category as well. Forty-one churches at or above one hundred members, and four dystrophic churches under one hundred members. Size is not the determinate factor. There are five critical factors determining the stability that exert the most pressure toward dystrophy: reliance on pastor and paid staff, a high proportion of resources poured into the building and grounds, high levels of inactivity or "representative" ministry,[1] low or no awareness of the true impact of ministry and programs, and little or no membership accountability.

Many of our larger growing churches are on the verge of sliding toward decay. The growth that allowed them to expand, build, and relocate is ebbing, as is their attendance and giving. The number of inactive members explodes. One church in this survey carries over 1,000 names of people who haven't attended worship in over three years and make no annual contribution, and it is only a matter of time until this level of inactivity begins to erode the overall health of the congregation.

Some of the premiere large churches in United Methodism set a standard for activity that is incredible. These churches are active seven days a week, offer multiple worship and learning experiences, provide various services to the members and community, and are reaching an ever expanding number of new people. Some of the participants in these churches tell amazing stories of how their lives have been transformed since they joined. Some of these churches make the gospel accessible to thousands of people in worship, through radio and television broadcasts, webcasts, podcasts, and a host of innovative electronic and paper media.

There is nothing wrong with being big, unless "bigness" becomes a standard by which you judge effectiveness. Once "big" becomes a goal, it ceases to inspire and it begins to oppress. As a denomination of smaller congregations (75% of United Methodist congregations have fewer than 150 members), it is a disservice to hold forth as models, examples, or "teaching churches"—congregations that beat all the odds. As will become evident, some of our largest churches must ascribe a significant part of their success to factors beyond the control of most local congregations—location, the charisma or skill-set of an appointed pastor, or unique funding sources, to name a few—and therefore their success is not transferable to other settings. For a generation, we have been enamored with the "we did it, you can do it too!" success stories of the megachurch. Some of these stories are valid, but some are not.

---

1. Representative ministry exists where a few people provide a ministry for the church, while the majority of participants remain uninvolved. Many people feel they are participating in the ministry by contributing money, goods, or offering prayers. This passive involvement results in representative ministry.

Dystrophic congregations demand the most from their leaders. It takes an enormous amount of time, money, energy, expertise, and other resources to run a fast growing church. Most dystrophic churches hire an excessive number of paid staff to make sure everything runs smoothly. Many pastors of the dystrophic congregations in this study confess that they serve primarily as "CEOs" and "tenth trustees," often putting in sixty, seventy, and eighty-plus hours a week to direct the administrative life of the congregation. The drive and energy of the pastors and laity leadership of some of our largest congregations constantly amazed me.

My critique of dystrophic congregations is simply this: most of them are too dependent on a few factors, making them highly unstable, and therefore unsustainable. In no less than twenty-five churches, the pastor told me some variation of the following comment, "I can't leave here because the minute I do everything will fall apart." In many cases, one or two "deep-pocket givers" provided a substantial portion of the church's annual income. If, for some reason, they withheld their giving, the church would suffer greatly. At least forty of the churches in the sample had enjoyed two of three decades of growth due to their location, but already they are feeling the pinch as the population migrates in different directions.

Every dystrophic congregation can work on the sustainability issues, but they pose some unique and controversial challenges. Of the four church types, the largest percentage of "passive" participants exists in the dystrophic category. What this means is that many people are drawn to large churches because they have low standards for engagement, offer high anonymity, and they appeal to the consumeristic "pick and choose" mentality. When congregations increase the demands on participants, when they begin to hold one another accountable, and when they balance outreach, witness, and service with worship, small groups, and fellowship, many people choose to leave, looking for someplace else that expects less. Many dystrophic church leaders desire greater stability and sustainability, but without having to lose numbers in the process. This may be impossible. Every vital church in the study described a period of membership/participant decline when they got serious about Christian discipleship.

Sense of Identity

The leaders of dystrophic congregations have a strong, clear sense of identity. Ask anyone in a leadership position, "Who are you?" and you will get a fairly good answer. Move outside of the inner circle, however, and things begin to get fuzzy. In an inordinate number of growing churches, it is the vision, drive, and ambition of the senior pastor that defines the identity of the congregation. Dystrophic congregations are unique in one significant way: They are often referred to not by their name, but by the pastor's. Pastors of both dystrophic and decaying congregations freely refer to the congregation they serve as "my church," or "my ministry"; something virtually no pastor of a vital or retrogressive congregation ever does. (They refer to the church in the plural: "our church" or "our ministry.")

Another characteristic of dystrophic congregations is for members and leaders to describe it in terms of what it does rather than who it is. Ask a leader of a dystrophic congregation who they are and generally you receive a litany of programs, ministries, and worship options. It is often difficult to cut through all the activities to find out what the core values, critical beliefs, and sense of call is that generates all of the programmatic activity. *"Being"* is superseded by *"doing."* Almost every pastor of a dystrophic congregation can navigate the intricate distinctions between the doing and being aspects of the church, but most congregational leaders and staff are not as savvy. It is often difficult to gain a clear sense of the identity of many dystrophic churches.

Interviews with people who attend these churches are enlightening. Answers to the question, "How would you describe the identity of this church?" tended to reflect the growth aspects, rather than sustainability:

"Big, fun, exciting!"

"The more we get [to attend], the more we can do. The more we can do, the more we attract [new people]."

"Worship isn't boring. It's the best hour of my week."

"God is love, and people don't have to do anything to receive it."

"It has great music."

"We welcome anyone who walks in the door."

"No pressure to join. Come as you are."

"We have the best music program in town, and the prettiest sanctuary."

"We have the best preacher money can buy."

"There is something for everyone at this church. You'll never be bored."

"It is a great church—there isn't an empty seat in the house."

These are representative of hundreds of comments—some coming close to talking about what the church believes, but mostly about what it offers in terms of program or worship. These comments would not be remarkable if they weren't so different from those made about retrogressive and vital congregations.[2] It is also important to note that the number one answer to the question of identity was, "I really don't know."

Shared Clarity of Purpose

After "Who are we?" the second most important question is, "Why are we here?" As with the sense of identity, clarity of purpose tends to be high within the leadership of the local church, but increasingly fuzzy the further from the leaders you go.

The operative word in dystrophic congregations is "more": more people, more program, more money, more building, and more staff. Analyzing the planning and goal setting of dystrophic congregations, it is striking that they generally target increasing membership, raising money, expanding or remodeling the building, launching new programs, or hiring new staff (often to tend to ministries that no laity will step forward to lead). To be fair, most of the leaders see growth as the primary means of reaching people with the gospel, but often it is assumed that one will automatically lead to the other. Many dystrophic congregations are doing no more than an average job of helping existing participants grow in their faith and spiritual life, yet they believe that the key to effectiveness is getting more new people to join. Faith formation, while often articulated as the primary goal, is secondary to congregational growth in actual fact.

"Growth" is a confusing term in the church, because we use the single word to refer to both quantitative increase, as well as qualitative improvement. The less sustainable the church, the more likely it is that the quantitative definition of growth will be used. More sustainable congregations use the qualitative definition. There is strong evidence that the consumeristic orientation of the United States culture affects our expectations and priorities in the church. When the cultural messages are "bigger is better," "the one with the most toys wins," and "winning is everything," it is no surprise that the church adopts similar ways of thinking. Dystrophic congregations display an amazing amount of competitive spirit.

2. More will be said in chapters 3 and 4, but the most common comments in stable congregations relate to the number of people's lives touched, and the needs met. "This church is committed to becoming Christlike and it is a place where I encounter God, feel the empowerment of the Holy Spirit, and am equipped to use my gifts to share God's love with the world." This is the quality and character of the answers to the same question about identity in vital and retrogressive churches.

Being the biggest, most active, and most "successful" church is a common goal of many dystrophic churches. Many of the congregations in this study regularly compare themselves with other churches in the area. One quote from a pastor in the southeast epitomizes the "win at any cost" mentality of many dystrophic congregations: "Our driving goal—our vision for the future—is to be the biggest church. Not just in the conference, not just in the city, not just in the state. We are planning to become the biggest church in North America. We look at every church within forty miles as our competition—even other United Methodist churches—especially the large evangelical independents. We are prepared to invest everything we have in becoming a cutting edge, state-of-the-art, nationally-known, megachurch." The pastors, paid staff, and elected leadership of this congregation developed a comprehensive strategic plan, all carefully designed to continuously expand. The lay leader of this church exudes both confidence and excitement when he adds, "We have a goal of 50,000 worshipers by 2030, with a television viewership of over one million. We are following the success stories of the Willow Creeks and Saddlebacks to become a one-of-a-kind church."

On one level, such incredible goals are exciting, but on another level they raise serious questions. How effectively can one congregation attend to the spiritual formation needs of over a million people? At what point do the institutional and organizational demands preclude the missional and spiritual needs of the church? What is the ultimate value of such a large congregation? How will the world be better due to the size and influence of such a church? One leader of this congregation told me that these questions were of little concern. She said, "Our purpose is to grow—every day to bring one or more people into the church. What happens to them then is between them and God."

I use this extreme story to illustrate a simple point: clarity of purpose is important, but not just any purpose. Leaders of congregations who believe that the institution of the church is the most important thing create unstable and unsustainable congregations. The local church is a means to an end, not an end in itself. It is never enough to grow the congregation, but rather to equip each congregation to *be* the church in the world.

The Focus of the Congregation

Obviously, the predominant focus is inward in dystrophic congregations. When the majority of a congregation's efforts are to attract more people to attend worship and programs, when the majority of funds go into the building, staff, and maintenance of the existing church, and when the prevailing plan is to continually expand the participating membership, then very little attention is focused outward.

This is not to say that dystrophic churches do not do a lot of good work beyond the congregation. However, this focus is isolated and sporadic. A few committees, work teams, and small groups provide outreach ministry in the name of the whole congregation. Many of the largest congregations are rightfully proud of their ministries to the homeless and hungry, their mission teams, their food pantries, soup kitchens, and thrift shops, as well as work in clinics, prisons, hospitals, and nursing homes. Yet on closer inspection, the number of participants who engage in these ministries represent a small segment of the congregation. These pockets of vitality exist in every dystrophic church I visited, but they do not make the whole church vital.

The vast majority of attendees at worship in dystrophic congregations are not interested in the inward-outward focus question—they are mostly interested in what the congregation has to offer them personally. Dystrophic churches have great appeal to those with a passive, consumeristic mindset. Polling thousands of participants in large churches in Ohio, Florida, Texas, North Carolina, California, Kansas, and Georgia, a clear and overwhelming message emerged. Eighty-one percent (3,794 of 4,684 polled) stated that their "total involvement with the church was attending a worship service." This was a completely random sampling of those leaving the church service, and while it is not a statistically significant sample, I believe it is an honest representation of those most drawn to our fastest growing churches—they attend to have personal, individual needs met.

Indeed, worship, small groups, and a wide variety of midweek programs in dystrophic congregations tend to focus on the individual. Self-help groups, sermons, Bible studies, and programs attract many people to the church. Theological depth is sacrificed for cultural breadth in dystrophic congregations. As one pastor related, "People do not need to come to church to feel bad about themselves. Church should be a port in the storm, a relief from all the negativity. I know some people say that you should challenge people when they come to church, but that's a turn-off. When people leave this church, they feel good about themselves. We have made a name for ourselves as the church of unconditional love."

The focus of most dystrophic churches is on building the congregation at the general level, and on serving the individual in the messages they proclaim and the programs they offer.

Awareness and Understanding of God's Vision for the Church

Vision is a hot topic in dystrophic congregation. The question is, "Whose vision are we talking about?" Most leaders in dystrophic churches talk about their vision for ministry. Many tell stories of forming a vision team, working a visioning process, or that their pastor gave his or her vision to the church.[3] Few dystrophic congregations talk about prayer, discernment, or study of Scripture in relation to vision. Most dystrophic congregations have vision statements framed on a wall or printed in their bulletins and newsletters. All too often, leaders of the church cannot repeat the vision unless they have a copy in front of them. This reveals a fundamental flaw in understanding vision.

Compelling, transformative vision tends to be written in people's hearts, not on pieces of paper. They also tend to be vibrant, comprehensive, and inspiring images of a future in which almost anyone can picture him- or herself. One measure of a vision's power is how widespread it is. In dystrophic congregations, most people beyond the inner circle of leadership are unaware that the church even has a vision.

Dystrophic churches do a wonderful job of aligning what they do with their vision. Programs, worship services, ministries, community involvement, and the use of property and funds are solid reflections of the congregation's vision. In almost every setting they are designed to result in growth, and obviously they are effective. Effective dystrophic congregations have become expert at painting pictures, developing images, and drawing on compelling metaphors attractive to a wide variety of people. Many growing congregations use picture language, storytelling, and vision to create their public persona. Many members,

3. One significant observation to make of dystrophic congregations is that their senior pastors are predominantly male. Of the 234 dystrophic congregations, 218 have men as their senior pastors. Only sixteen women (7%) head dystrophic churches. Contrast this with thirty-one of sixty-nine (45%) vital churches, twenty of fifty-one (39%) retrogressive churches, and 188 of 363 (52%) decaying churches being led by women pastors.

regular participants, and visitors relate that it is this proficiency at telling stories that is the main attraction to the church.

Governing and Guiding Values

The values of dystrophic congregations exist on two parallel levels: articulated values and expressed values. Articulated values are what we *say* is important, while expressed values are evident by what we actually *do*. The leaders in dystrophic congregations talk a lot about leading people to Christ. It is very important to provide a place where people can meet to worship God, learn about their faith, and grow spiritually. There is no doubt that leaders in these churches want to honor God and further the work of Christ.

However, much more energy and time is spent in administrative functions, planning, programming, funding, staffing, marketing, equipping, and organizing than in moving out into the community.

One very simple distinction between stable and unstable congregations is in answer to the question: "How well do the values of the key leaders of this congregation reflect the wider values of the whole congregation?" In both decaying and dystrophic congregations, the leaders claim either that they think their values are different from the majority of the congregation or they really don't know what the congregation's values are. The main difference identified in dystrophic congregations is that leaders feel that their values result in a deeper level of commitment and support in the congregations, while the majority of members hold values that look for the ways they may benefit from the church without feeling a need to participate in its leadership. In both vital and retrogressive congregations, there is a strong certainty that values are shared throughout the entire community of faith.

Impact Awareness

The single most significant issue facing dystrophic congregations is the almost complete lack of awareness of the value of their ministries. This lack of knowledge arises from the fact that dystrophic congregations measure success in terms of numbers rather than transformation. As long as attendance is good, people continue joining, and money flows, dystrophic congregations assume they are doing a good job.

When asked how people's lives are being changed, how behaviors alter, how the community and world benefits through the thoughts, words, and actions of congregational participants, the vast majority of dystrophic church leaders have no clear answers. Some individual leaders tell stories of how their participation in the church changed their lives, but these stories are isolated. Many leaders of dystrophic congregations responded negatively to my question, "How do you measure a person's spiritual development and assess their progress toward Christlike-ness?" Three out of four leaders chided me for "judging" people, and a similar proportion told me that the answer to the question is "between the individual and God." In very few dystrophic churches did the leadership see any connection between such a qualitative measurement and the ability to improve their ministries.[4]

The most prevalent measure of effectiveness in dystrophic congregations is worship attendance. Even though most dystrophic congregations are growing in membership, they also have a large, and growing, number of people who attend worship (or another programmatic offering of the church) but never join. While giving is another quantitative measure used by dystrophic church leaders, it is not as reliable an indicator of growth due to the number of alternative funding sources, investments, endowments, and special gifts and loans. The centerpiece of life in a dystrophic church, and the fundamental measure of success, is the worship experience,[5] where you find the vast majority of participants.

The problem that dystrophic churches face in lacking an awareness of impact can be illustrated by a few quotes from disaffected participants:

"I attended this church for six years. I was welcomed, I was active and busy, I rarely missed a week—and I woke up one day and realized, I don't know God any better today than when I first started attending."

"If I miss a Sunday, I get, like, a half dozen phone calls and a card from the pastor. I attend regularly so that they'll leave me alone."

4. It has been incredibly heartening that a number of churches (almost one hundred) have sought some guidance and instruction in how to develop such metrics. This is one more piece of evidence that many leaders of dystrophic congregations would rather lead vital churches. They acknowledge that gaining impact awareness is one of the critical conditions to increasing stability.

5. This is true of both decaying and dystrophic congregations; the centerpiece of retrogressive churches is service opportunities, while spiritual formation in accountability group settings is the centerpiece of the vital church.

"I'm good as long as the music and preaching is good. I looked for a long time to find a church that wouldn't pester me to join or give. I get real nervous when a church starts licking its chops and sees me as a candidate for some committee. I left my last church for that reason. I come here because no one expects anything from me."

"I only come here about four times a year, and that's okay. It is so great finding a church that fits my lifestyle."

"I want to be a good person, and going to church helps me do that. My work life and home life are murder; I need a place to come to get away from all the crap. Church here is all about me."[6]

Sharing these comments with leaders in these churches meets with an interesting reaction. In almost every case the response was some form of, "too bad, that's their problem. We can only do so much, if people don't take advantage of it, there isn't much we can do about it." One leader characterized it this way, "We toss the bait in the water, we have no control over whether they bite or not."

Leadership

Layers of leadership characterize dystrophic congregations, though pastors exert an inordinate amount of power and influence. Often, both clergy and laity report that the church could not continue to be successful were the pastor to be removed. For this reason, many dystrophic congregations use their size and influence to guarantee that they can keep their pastor, some even withholding apportionments unless a promise is made to leave the pastor alone. Unfortunately, this is not rare, and it is growing in frequency as a church reaches the one-thousand-member mark.

Beyond the appointed pastor or pastoral team, dystrophic churches hire an exceptional number of paid professional staff members. For some churches, it is a badge of honor to have a large paid staff. This can be either a good or a bad thing. Many dystrophic churches hire staff to organize and equip the lay membership for ministry. This is a healthy use of staff. More often, however, staff are hired not to equip ministry, but to do ministry for the congregation that the membership is unwilling to do for itself. This is decidedly *not* healthy, but widespread.

6. These five quotes come from participants at five of the largest and most "successful" United Methodist churches, all identified as "Teaching Churches." They are not isolated, but representative, comments. The larger the congregation, the greater the population of people nominally connected to the community of faith.

Dystrophic congregations often approach leadership as an us/them enterprise. Pastor and paid staff find themselves disconnected from, or worse, at odds with, the elected laity leadership of the local congregation. Often, Boards of Trustees, Staff-Parish Relations Committees, and Church Councils are unaware of the work of the staff, and, in a few cases, the pastor. Many congregations live in a constant tension of "who's really in charge?"

Using the model of leadership as "the combination of visioning, futuring, and management,"[7] the following question was posed to the leaders in dystrophic congregations: "Who has primary responsibility for the three levels of leadership?" When meeting with paid staff, they claimed that their primary work is "Visioning/Futuring," and that the elected laity leadership more appropriately focused on "Management, with some attention to Futuring." Speaking to the elected leadership, they claimed that "Visioning/Futuring" was their province, while paid staff should deal with the "Management" issues. According to *The Book of Discipline*, the elected laity leadership are correct, though that is rarely followed in dystrophic congregations. The very existence of this disagreement about roles presents a significant challenge in many dystrophic congregations.

Another struggle in most dystrophic congregations is commitment of volunteers elected to various committees, boards, councils, and teams. Having so many people to choose from, it would seem that large churches would not have the same problem as small churches finding warm bodies to serve in leadership positions. This is not the case. Four out of five dystrophic congregations report a struggle with the nomination and election process each year. Only about 10% of the total congregation fills some leadership role, with between fifteen and twenty people filling multiple key roles. Attendance at scheduled meetings is sporadic, generally only about 60% of elected members show up to any meeting.

A United Methodist bishop commented on this situation in most large churches: "Not everyone is a leader. It is better to have a few good leaders than a lot of less gifted people attempting to do things they really can't do well. In my whole ministry, I was lucky to have a dozen people in any church that offered good leadership. I surrounded myself with those people. It worked for Jesus and it worked for me." A small core group of leaders is common in dystrophic congregations. Even when Church Councils number in the fifties, sixties, or higher, the real decision making occurs in a much smaller group.

7. See footnote 6 in chapter 1.

"It is one of the drawbacks of a large church," one pastor laments. "Everyone wants a voice at the table, and there are so many competing agendas. It is vitally important to make sure everyone has their say, but when all is said and done, you have to know who's accountable. Lots of people think the pastor shouldn't have so much power and control, but it is the pastor who is ultimately responsible for everything. I have to find people I can trust to work with, and that generally means a small inner circle."

Another perspective illustrates a deeply held truism: a church is only as good as its leadership. "We have got to have only the best people making decisions if we want to grow. We made a decision a while back that 'volunteer' could not equal 'amateur.' We need a certain level of expertise, not just willingness or desire. Some churches think that all you need is someone to say 'yes' when asked to serve. Our church believes that you need only those people committed to excellence."

This commitment to excellence contributes to the reliance on paid staff. Paid staff do tend to be held to higher standards of performance, but most churches report a boomerang effect; that is, fewer laity are willing to pitch in to do ministry that others are paid to do. Many pastors and laity leaders of dystrophic congregations complain that a large number of participants are only interested in being served, and these leaders realize that paying staff has a dis-empowering influence, but they feel trapped. Without highly motivated laity to step in and volunteer, the churches can ill afford to let staff go. In many cases, continued growth depends on paid professional staff.

Paid staff positions cover the whole gamut of church needs—choir directors, organists, musicologists, custodians, plant engineers, youth workers, young adult workers, older adults workers, program coordinators, evangelism specialists, business administrators, counselors, kitchen coordinators, events coordinators, hosts and hostesses, landscapers, interior designers, worship art specialists, potters, parking lot attendants, on-site health care specialists, caterers, bakers, printers, fund-raisers, writers, media specialists, and sound and light-board specialists are just a sample.

The Role of the Appointed Pastor(s)

Of all the churches in the sample, by far the largest number of multi-appointment churches are dystrophic. Generally, the senior pastor fills two major roles: CEO of the organization and primary preacher. Beyond the senior pastor, roles get a little fuzzy. Many associate pastors fulfill a support role, having responsibility for the program and elected laity leadership (senior pastors usually relate to paid staff). Some specialize in education, member care, or spiritual formation, but they have nominal power and influence compared to the senior pastor.

Dystrophic churches have a host of third-level pastors; for example: youth pastors, visitation pastors, pastoral care specialists, young adult pastors, outreach and evangelism pastors, and even an emerging projects pastor in one setting. Many of these are part-time, some retired, and a few work for more than one congregation.

Senior pastors have both the lion's share of responsibility as well as authority. It is not unusual for the senior pastor of a large congregation to work seventy-plus hour weeks. Those pastors identified by the denomination as "successful" add writing, teaching seminars, leading workshops, and all the necessary travel time to already overloaded schedules of preaching, teaching, attending meetings, and organizational and administrative duties. About half of the senior pastors in the sample report some distress at the demands that a growing church makes on them. They wish there was some way to relinquish some of the stress and demand, without losing power. Others report that growing churches create as many problems as they solve. Power plays, conflict, resistance to change, and fragmentation of the congregation all generate "fires" for the senior pastor to put out.

However, most pastors of dystrophic congregations thrive on the challenge. Many pastors have worked hard to grow their congregations, and they willingly give whatever time, energy, and effort is necessary to judge themselves successful. There is a strong sense of call and purpose for the pastors of growing churches. The blend of gifts, skills, knowledge, personal charisma and ambition usually result in a growing congregation.

"I wouldn't do anything else," confesses one pastor. "This is everything I ever dreamed of in ministry—a large congregation in a beautiful building offering just about any ministry you can think of. I have a beautiful home, and wonderful family, and if I'm lucky, another twenty-five years here. I wouldn't even leave this to become a bishop!"

Programmatic Design

Dystrophic churches are programmatic smorgasbords. Though they offer a wide variety of programs, they tend to cluster in five distinct categories: worship, small groups, congregational constituent groups, community constituent groups, and events.

Worship speaks for itself, but dystrophic congregations spearhead alternative worship options, dividing worship into traditional, contemporary, praise, contemplative, and indigenous "styles." Worship is viewed as the primary entry point into the life of the congregation, and is often identified as the optimal place to appeal to a new audience. Dystrophic churches approach the worship experience in one of two major ways—the first is to create an auditorium space capable of holding hundreds (if not thousands) of people at one time; the second is to offer multiple worship options for smaller congregations. Of course, some churches offer both, but building limitations often push churches to opt for the second choice, when they would prefer the first.

Because worship is the time each week when the largest number of people gather, worship in dystrophic congregations tends to be very "busy." Visitors find themselves greeted multiple times by a variety of people, announcements and pertinent information is projected in the narthex or on screens in the sanctuary, music is playing or is being performed. In the course of an hour, multiple choirs or bands may play, drama may be performed, Scriptures may be read or enacted, movie clips may be shown on mounted screens, special announcements given, a message offered (a sermon only in traditional services), prayers prayed for the congregation, and participants invited to some form of refreshment and/or fellowship immediately following the service.

It is the rare dystrophic church that does not have an active small group ministry. Small groups became the rage *du jour* of the late 1990s and have carried into the twenty-first century. A number of megachurches gained their amazing numbers through an intensive and well-planned small group ministry. Most dystrophic churches claim that there is a group for everyone, and if there isn't, they'll start one.

At the heart of small group ministry is a lately realized paradox of large churches, which is that most people come to church for a sense of intimacy and strong relationships. Commitment to the community of faith requires a deep sense of connection that comes to most people through relationships. The anonymity and individualistic focus of most large church worship experiences makes small groups essential. People need a place where they can wrestle with big questions of faith, God, life, purpose, and meaning—where they can share from the heart, and hear from others struggling with similar issues.

Dystrophic congregations understand that not everyone is at a place in their faith where wrestling with big issues is reasonable. For that reason, less demanding small groups are prevalent in some of the fastest growing churches—book groups, gardening clubs, rants (where people vent feelings about world events), luncheon groups, Starbucks coffee clubs, golfing small group ministries, (also, fishing, driving, shooting, shopping, insert-favorite-hobby-here), after-work social groups, etc. Sanctioned and supported by the church, these are called ministries of the church, though the focus isn't specifically on God, Christ, or the Christian faith.

The something-for-everyone mentality has both positives and negatives. The obvious positive is that people who would not otherwise darken the door may be attracted to a church exercise program, financial planning seminar, or yoga class. It broadens the number of entry points and opens the possibility of a long-term relationship. On the negative side, it generates a "shopping mall" image, which may be at odds with the integrity of a faith community. An unreported statistic for most growing churches is "dropaways." A dropaway is a participant who is extremely active in the initial phase of their relationship to the congregation, but involvement wanes over time, leading to inactivity. Dozens of pastors from dystrophic congregations resonate with this trend and share their own stories:

"It's true that we receive, on average, fourteen members each month, but only about four of them remain active beyond twelve months. The number of nominally active members in our church is growing faster than the actual membership," one pastor confesses. Another adds, "I have attended Large Church seminars for the past three years, and whenever I bring up this topic, I find that most of the pastors are nodding their heads in agreement. We've increased our membership by 20% in two years, worship attendance by almost a third, but our inactives are fast approaching 50% of the total congregation."

More than a few pastors are not concerned by the dropaway phenomenon. One senior pastor speaks for many when he says, "It is better for a person to have a church relationship, whether they attend or not. It says something that they made the effort to take vows in the first place. It reflects the world in which we live. Not everyone has time to come to church every week. Membership means more than just attending worship. It is what is in people's heart that matters most."

Reflecting on the issue of impact awareness, this attitude falls short. Most leaders in dystrophic congregations are ignorant of what is in people's hearts, whether participants are active or inactive. What does seem to matter to many dystrophic churches is that membership numbers stay large and growing. Actual attendance is secondary.

Organizational Structure

Dystrophic congregations are amazingly well organized, structured, and planned. The complexity of some of our largest congregations is truly amazing. In my files I have one organizational chart of a church with over 600 discreet positions with 150 lines of accountability, and the church runs like a well-oiled machine. Corporate America could learn much about organization from some of our dystrophic models.

The key question is not whether or not they are well organized, but what are they organized to do? The answer, in its simplest form, is that the best-organized dystrophic churches are organized to grow. They are designed to generate more interest, more involvement, more money, more program, and more activity, and they succeed mightily.

However, they often measure their success not by evaluating impact, but by gauging the increase of inputs. In the church, money, people, plant, and program are all inputs that are combined to deliver witness, nurture, and service to the community and world. The truest measure of a church's value is how the community and world improve because of its existence. Most dystrophic congregational leaders are unable to evaluate this impact, but they are ready, willing, and able to share attendance, giving, and membership figures.

As one disillusioned pastor of a fast growing church framed it, "It's like we are a luxury car, designed to hold and burn fuel, with a powerful engine, luxurious interior, top-of-the-line equipment, but no wheels. We don't go anywhere. We just sit here idling away in total comfort. I built this thing, but I can't get it to move!"

The majority of dystrophic churches are well crafted, and they are run in professional, businesslike ways. Professionals in business, finance, law, marketing, management, planning, and government serve on their boards and staffs. Once a church grows to a certain point (generally beyond 1,500 members), there are few things it could not accomplish, due to the intellectual capital, experience, and contacts from which it has to draw. There is very little to fault in the organizational expertise of most dystrophic congregations.

Money

How much money does a dystrophic church need? More. Just the costs of maintaining facility, paying staff, and insurance in a large church are greater than the total budgets of most United Methodist congregations. While three-quarters of our churches think in terms of tens-of-thousands of dollars, fast growing churches think first it terms of hundreds-of-thousands, then millions, of dollars. Weekly giving (the main focus of most decaying congregations) becomes one of many funding sources of the large church. Alternative income streams are generated through investments, endowments, rentals (for donations), high-end fundraising, donor cultivation, specialized funds, and planned giving. These alternative streams are available to all of our churches, but dystrophic congregations have become highly proficient at utilizing them to cover ever-escalating costs and fiscal needs.

The major benefit to this skilled level of funding ministry is that most dystrophic congregations are fiscally sound, asset rich, with a healthy cash flow. It is not until growth begins to level off that dystrophic churches feel the pinch. This pinch comes because participant giving is not closely tied to spiritual formation and steward development.[8] The downside of a broad funding base is that many people feel that the church doesn't need their money. A paradox that all churches face is that in a commodity-based culture, people are empowered to give when there is need, disempowered when needs are met. Very few unstable churches plan from an abundance base, where leadership figures out how to spend surplus funds. The majority of our churches use a cost basis, deciding first what to do, then figuring out how to raise the money to finance it. In congregations where the funding base depends on alternative sources, many givers do not feel a need to give.

As in decaying congregations, dystrophic church leaders spend an unwarranted amount of time talking about money, but for very different reasons. In decaying churches, money is a means to survival; there is often a desperation attached to money talk. In dystrophic congregations, money is a critically important tool for growth. Conversation about how to use and leverage money replaces discussion about how to get money. Money talk in dystrophic congregations tends to be strategic in nature.

The level of financial expertise and management potential in our largest churches could be a valuable asset to many struggling churches, and even to some of our Annual Conferences. I visited many congregations with capital reserves in the millions of dollars. The interest from any one of these funds could cover the annual budget of any number of struggling congregations. In some cases, where dystrophic congregations were beginning a slide toward

---

8. See giving comparisons in appendix 3.

decay, these funds were viewed as the church's hedge against the future; that is, the way they would be able to keep their doors open long after the number of giving units dropped below sustainability. In these rare cases, the power and role of money in the congregation changed dramatically. For the most part, money is viewed as the primary means of mission and ministry—the way to expand plant, staff, program, and outreach. As a tool, dystrophic congregations maximize the money potential to strengthen their church.

The Role of Worship in the Life of the Congregation

For dystrophic congregations, worship is central. Dystrophic churches have driven the worship revolution of the past thirty years. Almost every innovation, trend, fad, or new style of worship emerged from a dystrophic congregation. One reason for this is the fact that many dystrophic churches resulted from the efforts and designs of entrepreneurial Baby Boomers. Not content with "traditional" worship, Boomers pushed beyond the status quo to test many "contemporary" forms and styles of worship. The impact of Baby Boomers' tastes and preferences rocked mainline churches in the late twentieth century, and are defining the neo-tradition for the early twenty-first. Worship is less interactive, relying much more on performance art. Music, drama, dance, video, readings, fabric art, and metaphor are presented to gathered worshipers. Many praise songs are performed for the assembled group. Singing along is impossible with the stylized performance of the song leaders. Gone in many settings are responsive readings, affirmations of faith, unison readings of Scripture, unison prayers, personal testimony, and invitations to leave the pew (for communion, altar call, offering), and in some cases even an offering, doxology, or the sharing of the Lord's Prayer. Abbreviated communion and baptism rituals remove congregational response, or limit them to a minimum. While a traditional option is generally retained, most of the energy and effort moves to the newly emerging worship styles.

Many dystrophic congregations set worship attendance goals as their primary performance measures. "We have a team of people whose entire purpose is to answer the question: 'How do we get them in the door of the sanctuary?' We have a vision of our sanctuary filled with people at least once every day of the week, with multiple worship experiences on Saturday and Sunday," one lay ministries director reports. "We can easily seat 4,000 people and we want to have 20,000 people worshiping with us within five years. By the end of the next decade, we hope to have 50,000 worshipers each and every week." Further plans for how to integrate these worshipers into the larger life of the church are not even discussed. Getting them in is the main thing.

I want to be careful not to sound contemptuous of these goals. While they may be incomplete, they arise from a genuine desire to help people hear the gospel of Jesus Christ. The leaders of worship in every dystrophic congregation I attended have a deep personal love of God and a desire to see their church thrive and grow. At no time do I want to insult the integrity of the men and women who see worship as central in these congregations.

On the other side, the pew-sitter side, however, it is important to evaluate how this centrality of worship is often interpreted. A significant number of people who attend these large, growing churches have an active spiritual life, and worship is just one aspect of their faith formation; but the greatest number of people who occasionally attend a worship service as their only church involvement attend dystrophic churches. Repeatedly, I heard one form or another of the statement; "I like this church because all I have to do is attend worship when I want to." Worship becomes the bar of low expectations that many people think they need to clear in order to be right with God. Many dystrophic congregational leaders do little or nothing to dissuade people of this notion. In fact, many leaders from dystrophic churches defended the notion that attending worship is "good enough." "We can't know what is going on in an individual's personal relationship with God. There are many roads to salvation. We are just glad that we can be here when they need us," was a sentiment echoed by a large number of these church leaders.

The bottom line for most dystrophic churches is this: If we can do only one thing really well, we want it to be worship. Everything else is secondary.

The Role of Education in the Life of the Congregation

Christian education is important to dystrophic churches, but only in the broadest, most general sense. The sheer number of learning opportunities speaks volumes about the perceived importance of learning for all ages. Additionally, the focus on the importance of small groups for spiritual formation provides a wonderful context for lifelong learning.

Dystrophic congregations offer a wide variety of learning options, but few present lifelong learning as integral to the Christian life. Learning is an option, and each individual decides its importance. Two-thirds of all participants in dystrophic congregations opt out of any form of learning or Christian education. Leaders in the congregation rarely challenge such decisions.

These criticisms aside, dystrophic congregations offer a high quality of learning experience across the entire lifespan. I encountered interesting, well-taught, engaging, interactive classes, workshops, seminars, and retreats for little children, older children, youth, young adults, adults, and older adults in most of the churches in the survey. Equipping, training, and supporting churches is a high priority in many dystrophic congregations, and the integrity shows. I met many deeply committed, vibrant, and excited educators in some of our largest churches. More than in any other functional area, I encountered Christians who felt they were using their gifts and fulfilling their call to ministry through teaching and education. Of all the most hopeful signs in The United Methodist Church today, Christian education burns brightest and hottest. It is deeply encouraging.

What is missing in most dystrophic congregations is a master plan for learning. As with most decaying churches, the learning in dystrophic congregations doesn't seem to lead anywhere. There is rarely a sense of graduation, or a move from introductory courses to secondary to advanced to mastery and expert levels. Few dystrophic congregations have learning standards or criteria by which to judge an individual's growth and development. I found only one dystrophic church that helped participants develop a learning plan for spiritual development and faith formation.

So, while learning is important, it is subjective, sporadic, and hit-or-miss. One of the most striking differences between stable and unstable congregations exists in the make-up of Sunday school classes and Bible studies. In decaying and dystrophic congregations, classes are formed, people join, and the same people may stay in the same class for years, regardless of the topics, curriculum, or course content. In retrogressive and vital congregations, classes are formed around essential content, the best teachers and leaders are recruited to present the content, and participants move from class to class. In unstable congregations, fellowship exerts influence over content. In stable congregations, content drives the learning experience.[9]

---

9. A comparison table of Learning in the Four Church Types is found in appendix 4.

The Congregation's Relationship to the Community

Most dystrophic congregations go out of their way to develop positive relationships with the community in which they are located. For one reason, the community is the pool of potential new participants from which the congregation draws. For another reason, most leaders of dystrophic congregations are incredibly image conscious. They want their church to be well respected and widely known.

However, most leaders of larger churches do not want the church's success dependent on those outside the congregation. There is a strong "we'd rather do it ourselves" mentality in most dystrophic churches. "We want others to ask to partner with us," one pastor explained, "instead of the other way around."

A large number of dystrophic churches offer services to the community. Daycare, health centers, nursery schools, thrift shops, food pantries, Meals on Wheels, literacy programs, and coffee houses, are just a few of the common examples. Safe houses, crisis intervention centers, group homes, retreat centers, women's shelters, and financial planning and credit management are some of the more specialized ministries. These ministries are provided *for* the community, rather than *with* the community. They do an amazing amount of good for a huge number of people.

"We want to be the safety net for those who fall through the cracks," shares one pastor of a major metro church. "It is our goal to bridge the gaps left by Social Services and County Welfare. We have the facility, and the resources, and the staff to handle just about anything on a limited basis." When asked who else is involved in this work, she proudly proclaims, "No one. We do this all ourselves!" For churches large enough to do this well, it works just fine. However, it does not provide a model that many United Methodist churches can emulate. Too many dystrophic churches model autonomy over collaboration and cooperation.

Some dystrophic churches envision themselves as community centers. It works to the benefit of a growing church to have as many people as possible pass through the doors. Each person, regardless of the reason they enter the building, is a potential participant in the future life of the church. "We are committed to making every experience any person has in our church so positive that they would be crazy not to come back," emotes one energetic outreach director. "I want you to love this place so much that you want to be here all the time."

I visited with participants in senior's groups, ESL (English as a Second Language) groups, a youth basketball program, boy and girl scouts, 4H members, and a host of other clubs, groups, and gatherings, and heard ringing praises of the hosting churches. There is a deep appreciation and a wellspring of good feeling generated by opening the church doors to the community.

Some large church trustees tell another story. Acknowledging the importance of community connections, some leaders struggle with the liability issues and the negative wear-and-tear on the facilities. Insurance, security, ethical conduct, safety, and legal ramifications are priority concerns with the trustees of dystrophic churches. One gentleman shook his head and said, "If I had my way we'd lock the doors and kick 'em all out—but that wouldn't be very Christian would it?"

The Congregation's Relationship to the Connectional System

"Love/hate relationship" comes immediately to mind when examining the feelings about dystrophic church leaders with the Annual Conference and the United Methodist denomination. Many pastors and lay leaders sing the praises of the theology and polity of the church, of the connectional system, of the Wesleyan tradition, and the denomination's rich history. Voices falter when the topics turn to apportionments, the itineracy, or the intervention of district superintendents. Most leaders in dystrophic congregations share a similar viewpoint. "We will fulfill our conference obligations as long as the conference leaves us alone." An all-too-common confession of many large church leaders is that they are glad they have grown to the point where they have enough clout to get around the system. Many pastors speak of a "guaranteed appointment" as long as the church continues to grow. A few confess to financial leverage with the conference (i.e., apportionment payments amount to an insurance premium against moving the senior pastor). In a good number of cases, leaders in dystrophic churches say simply, "The conference does its thing, and we do ours."

Of the four church types, only dystrophic churches tend to downplay their denominational connection. In some cases, the church name eliminates "United Methodist" completely, or includes it only in very small letters. One high-profile pastor explained it to me this way: "We are in a very competitive market, where the independents have all the advantages. 'United Methodist' carries baggage that we don't need to deal with. Our ultimate purpose is not to make Methodists, but to make Christian disciples. As long as we introduce people to a relationship with God, it doesn't much matter what we call ourselves." The majority of pastors present at this gathering nodded their heads in agreement.

Most dystrophic pastors see a mutually beneficial, symbiotic relationship with the conference. As a denomination experiencing almost a full century of numeric decline, growing churches are a badge of honor to the annual conference. Success stories are few and far between. Pastors of large churches who write books, produce videos, speak at large gatherings, and teach workshops are fantastic public relations, for the pastor, for the pastor's church, and for the Annual Conference. Conferences that allow successful pastors long tenure ensure growth potential in the specialized setting. There are few advantages to moving a successful pastor from the congregation he or she builds up. It is only in very rare cases that a local church has to exert much pressure on a conference to leave the pastor in place.

Three bishops offer one other perspective. In a conversation with them about what it is like having "star performers" in their conferences, episcopal leaders confessed that it is, indeed, a mixed blessing. "We could use their gifts at the conference level," one lamented, "but they're too busy." Another said, "Our large churches got large by acting congregational, not connectional. It isn't worth the grief to butt heads with a big church. We really do tend to leave them alone." "It isn't that much of a hardship, except with the prima donnas, but there are only a couple of those. My only regret is that we need what they have to offer in other places, but we don't dare move them," the third added.

Dystrophic congregations reap what benefits they can from the connectional system, but in many significant ways, they operate independently. And with so many pressing challenges facing the church, it is easier leaving large congregations alone, rather than wasting time and energy warring with them over appointments.

Summarizing the Dystrophic Condition

Bigger has some definite advantages, but the jury is out on whether bigger is better. Many of our large congregations owe their growth to location, the charisma and leadership of the appointed pastor, or specialized funding sources, any of which could change and undermine the sustainability of the congregation's growth. There is nothing inherently *wrong* with a dystrophic church, but there is much that is *fragile*. The fortunes of a local congregation can change quickly, and the less attention given to stabilizing forces, the more dramatic those changes will be.

High levels of inactivity, low standards of membership and participation, a large number of paid staff, small numbers of participants in leadership, uneven giving patterns, an inward focus, and a "we can do it alone" mindset are some of the significant destabilizing factors that dystrophic congregations should address.

The creation of learning goals, spiritual formation plans, the integration of outward service with inward development, and equipping people to live their faith in the world are further stabilizing practices that would strengthen most dystrophic congregations.

Working against these stabilizing factors are two strong cultural forces: popularity and consumerism. Many of our growing churches are growing because they have mastered high-energy, low expectation experiences that make people feel good. Sharing the message is what they are all about. They maintain that what people do with the message they receive isn't their concern. But the long-term price of appealing to consumers may be too costly for The United Methodist Church to pay. Consumers are customers only as long as they value what is offered them. If the tastes change, the relationship ends. One pastor of a premiere large UM church confided, "We are like the queen in Alice in Wonderland, running as fast as we can to stay in one place. It is exhausting trying to stay anywhere near the cutting edge. Eventually we won't be in front any more, but a lot of my people don't understand that."

The intention of leaders in dystrophic congregations, from senior pastors through paid staff to elected congregational leaders, is to be a good church—to do good work for God, and to help people know the love of God. But size matters. Once a church gets to a certain size, a substantial amount of time, energy, and attention shifts to administration, organization, and structure. This shift changes the very nature of the church, affecting the congregation's sense of identity, purpose, and focus. A pastor who left the ministry from a "highly successful" church admitted, "My struggle was I kept confusing 'big' with 'faithful.' I thought because we were growing in numbers, it meant we were growing as Christians. What I ended up with was a lot of demanding people who had no real desire to be disciples. They just wanted to be served. It wasn't what I wanted, and it wasn't what I was called to, but somewhere along the way, it is what my ministry became."

Dystrophic congregations can gain the greatest benefit by shifting focus from quantity to quality—striving for balance, and seeking to develop evaluative metrics that allow them to better judge the impact value of their ministries and programs. Large, growing congregations do so much good, but there is not one church I visited that couldn't do more, and do it better. Churches that are making great strides toward greater stability and sustainability are those that are carefully examining their underlying assumptions—not just judging what they do, but unearthing the underlying values that explain *why* they do what they do.

CHAPTER THREE

The Retrogressive Congregation

I will confess that I find this to be the most fascinating of the four church types, though I am not sure it is a pure type. Retrogressive churches are highly focused, highly stable congregations that are losing participants. This condition can only exist for a short period of time. Either the focus of the congregation will begin to attract new participants, leading to growth and vitality, or numbers will continue to decline, eroding sustainability, leading to decay. Retrogressive congregations are in a transitive state, unlike the three other types.

Leaders from every retrogressive congregation share a similar threefold litany: simplify, prioritize, and focus. This is the very definition of the retrogressive church type: a church that makes the strategic and incredibly difficult decision to do just one or two things very well rather than a variety of things less well. Retrogressive congregations become known for their area of specialization. While this attractive to some, those seeking a wide variety of programs and ministries to choose from seldom find a home in the retrogressive church.

The most critical consideration of the leaders of retrogressive churches is not attracting new members, but the impact a narrower focus has on existing membership. As church leaders set priorities, eliminate long-standing programs, clarify focus, and strive to fully integrate participants into the ministry of the congregation, many church members decide they want something different.

For example, one inner city church decided to focus on ministry to older adults throughout the community. For years this church struggled to provide a full range of ministries and services as the existing membership aged. Despite best efforts and intentions, the church failed to draw many younger members, so that the children's and youth ministries eroded. As racial diversity increased in the neighborhood surrounding the church, the church dabbled in multicultural ministries, but with very little success. Many years of decline hurt the morale of the congregation and created constant problems for the leaders as they fought to do more and more with less and less.

Embarking on a long process of prayerful discernment and strategic planning, the leaders identified four ministries they did very well. They assessed their gifts and skills in each of the four areas, analyzed their available resources, evaluated the critical needs—both within and beyond the congregation—and honestly appraised where they could achieve the greatest effectiveness. Much agonizing deliberation led to their decision to focus on ministries to older adults throughout their community. Within months, the church became a community center for seniors. Health screenings, Meals on Wheels delivery, visitation, home repair projects, and counseling services were added to worship services, Bible studies, fellowship groups, prayer groups, and Sunday school classes—all aimed at fifty-five-and-older men and women. Out of this foundation emerged a soup kitchen, thrift shop, reading club, Habitat for Humanity team, and a host of other programs staffed by, organized with, and focusing on older adults. The pastor estimates that during the two years following this decision, the number of people served by the ministries of the church rose from about fifty to 500, while the membership fell from around eighty-five to sixty. About one-third of the members of the congregation chose to leave because they felt their church no longer served them. The lay leader of the church reflects, "We did not take our decisions lightly. We were in danger of dying and had to make some hard choices. There were heavy costs involved, but the benefits so far outweighed the costs that we know we did the right thing. When we tried to do a little of everything, we did very poorly and a lot of our people were inactive. Now that we do one thing really, really well, everyone is very involved and highly invested in our success. We are the best church for older adults in the entire conference, even though we're really small."

Retrogressive congregations are generally smaller, but exceptionally potent. Of all the churches in the sample, retrogressive congregations boast the highest levels of participation, the highest percentage of people engaged in ministry and leadership, and the highest per participant giving. They are a powerful reminder that a faith community does not need to be large to be successful. In fact, a number of one hundred member retrogressive congregations are making a larger impact on more lives than most churches ten times as large.[1]

Sense of Identity

Participants in retrogressive congregations have an *incredibly* strong sense of identity. The simplest explanation for this is that they are focused on just one or two areas of ministry. They know who they are because they are grounded in a very small set of values that define what they do and why they do it. The sense of community, connectedness, and commonality is deep in retrogressive churches.

"I was always on the periphery before. There were as many things going on I didn't care about as those I did in churches I attended before. Here, I fully and completely belong. I am engaged in all aspects of this congregation's life," reports a retired high school science teacher, "and I feel like it is really important that I am here. Not only am I growing as a Christian, but I am empowered to live as a Christian as well." This sense of centrality, of being a valuable part of the ministry, is widespread throughout retrogressive congregations.

"We don't have any 'passive participants' here," explained one pastor. "Every person in this church is in active ministry. You can ask any person here what their ministry is, and they will have an answer. We don't just print it in our bulletin. It's the truth: Our members are the ministers of this congregation." The level of active participation in retrogressive congregations is nothing short of phenomenal. Most can claim 100% participation, or close to it. "We don't measure how many people show up. We measure how many people share their faith in word or deed each week. You go pray with people at the hospital or work an hour at the soup kitchen or drive folks to their doctor's appointment.

---

1. Twelve congregations, randomly selected (three in each church type) were compared using a standard of "people served per participant per week." These acts of service are intentional, explicit, and reflect a conscious use of gifts as an expression of faith. Members of the twelve congregations developed the criteria by which they would be judged, and representatives of each church calculated their own results. The dramatic difference in scores reflects the discrepancy between stable and unstable congregations regarding "inactive" members. Higher percentages of inactive members greatly affect the scoring. Here are the results: Retrogressive: 4.3, Vital: 2.2, Decaying: 0.2, Dystrophic: 0.1.

That's as important (if not more important) than coming to worship on Sunday morning. Most of the people here? They do all four," shares the Ministries Coordinator of a 200+ member church. Two hundred people are active in ministry every week out of 200 members. Such incredible levels of participation don't happen by accident; they can only happen by design.

"When we had almost 500 members, we couldn't do what we're able to now," says the pastor. "Forgive me for being crass, but we were carrying way too much dead wood. The majority of people here didn't want to be *in* ministry; they wanted to be ministered *to*. There was only one way we could get from there (where we were) to here (where we are now), and that was to make membership mean something."

Making membership mean something is a high priority of all stable congregations, both retrogressive and vital. Clear standards of participation exist in the healthiest churches. Beyond the vague and general vows to support the church through "prayers, presence, gifts, and service,"[2] stable congregations flesh out specific expectations for people desiring to be full members of the church. How often should people pray? What is reasonable monetary giving behavior? What requirements for spiritual formation, Christian witness, and Christian service do church leaders expect? What precisely will people be measured against and held accountable to? These are questions to which every retrogressive and vital congregation has answers.

Of all the potentially controversial concepts in this book, establishing standards of membership and accountability will cause the greatest stir. The vast majority of our United Methodist churches shy away from holding members accountable for their actions (or inactions). For the most part, individual church members decide for themselves what it means to fulfill their vows. Failure to participate in most congregations results in little or no response from the church. Where there is no accountability, it is not unusual to find names of people listed as members who haven't participated in the church in years. Compare the lax standards of most churches with the following explanation of membership at a small, but stable, Midwestern church:

"If you want to be a member here you will engage in some form of corporate worship every week, you will pray daily, and pray at least once each week with others from the fellowship. You will attend a formation group, and you will engage in some form of outreach ministry every week. Every person will

---

2. Membership vows of The United Methodist Church.

connect with an ongoing ministry of the fellowship— giving time to plan, coor-
dinate, implement, and evaluate—regularly (like, as often as necessary to get
things done). We don't set a specific standard for giving, but we expect everyone to carry their own weight, and we challenge each other to give sacrificially
and regularly, which isn't a problem, since the majority of our people passed
10% a long time ago. For us, a tithe would be a low goal, so we don't talk about
it, except as a spiritual concept. That's what it takes to be a member. You stop
doing any of it for more than a week or two, and you're no longer a member.
It's that simple!"

The commitment to standards and accountability is a serious contributing
factor to the small and declining number of members. As one woman said of
her church shortly after it "imposed" standards on its members, "I didn't sign
up for this. I can go to any other church in the city and they won't make me do
any of this. I've loved this church since I was a girl, but there is no way I am
going to stay here and put up with this." Hers is not an uncommon response.
One pastor of a strong retrogressive congregation explains, "There are some
people around here who literally hate me, have said to me, 'Who do you think
you are?' and they complain that we have no right to hold them accountable to
their membership vows. But for the people who have stayed—who are living in
the new reality—they really like it; they like that being a Christian or a
Methodist actually means something." A youth member echoes her thoughts
when he says, "People are proud, you know? Being Christian is important now.
It's not easy, it's not optional, you can't just phone it in, it's cool. My friends are
like, 'You go to *that* church?' Whoa!"

"You ask who we are? We are a praying, serving, worshiping, learning,
leading body. Lots of churches say things like that, and it's true of some of the
people some of the time. But, us? It's true of all of us all the time. I have never
been in a church like this before," describes one woman from a newly-vital, for-
merly-retrogressive congregation. Her description is the rule, rather than the
exception, for retrogressive churches.

Shared Clarity of Purpose

Participants in retrogressive congregations know not only who they are, but
why they exist. They have as strong a sense of purpose as a sense of identity.
Leaders of these congregations are masters at answering the question, "What
can we do better than anything else?" Once they have the answer to this question,

they align every resource to this focus. In time, the church comes to identify itself by its sense of purpose. "We're the homeless church," or "We're the Bible study church," or "We're the street people church," are common responses. We are what we do.

The pursuit of a singular purpose in retrogressive churches is so strong that they are often known as well in their communities as they are by their own participants. Walk up to anyone in town and ask about these churches and you will here, "Oh, you mean the soup kitchen church," or "That's the church with all the great kids' ministries." Many people might not know the church by name, but they definitely know it by reputation of its good works.

One reason that participants in retrogressive congregations have no problem stating the purpose is that they represent the faithful remnant. Everyone who stays does so because they like and believe in what the church is doing. Those who have a different interpretation of what a church ought to do tend to leave these congregations. Newcomers decide to stay with the congregation based on how well they connect with the church's focus. A church with a simple, clear, concise purpose finds it much easier to get everyone on the same page.

Focus of the Congregation

The predominant focus of retrogressive congregations is outward—meeting an identified need of the community or a specific group within the community. In only two cases was the focus inward—on building spiritual community, but with an emphasis on performing acts of mercy and service for others.

By definition, the focus in retrogressive congregations is narrow, but deep. A retrogressive congregation may focus on meeting the needs of only one age group, but it provides everything needed for that age group. Those congregations focused on the poor and marginalized strive to meet those specific needs in a variety of ways.

The downside to such a strong, narrow, and deep focus is a lack of balance and diversity. One urban congregation deeply committed to the physical and spiritual needs of street people in their city works tirelessly to offer comfort and aid to those in need. Participants in this congregation give time, money, heart, and soul to the work, and spend much more time out on the street corners than in the church building. The problem (as *I* see it—leaders of this church don't see this as a problem) is they have virtually no time for Bible study, spiritual formation, or theological reflection. The lay leader said to me, "We know all the

Bible we need to: 'What does the LORD require of you? Seek mercy, do justice, and walk humbly with God.' Simple as 'do unto others.' Once we're finished being merciful, just, and kind, then we'll go back in and learn what to do next."

While narrowing focus and setting clear priorities are essential for the short term health of retrogressive congregations, the pathway to full vitality requires a balanced integration of both acts of piety and acts of mercy—inward spiritual development and outward practical service. Too narrow a focus for too long undermines the short-term benefits. The ability to be effective over time depends on the ability of a stable church to begin to grow. The vast majority of vital congregations report that they first had to experience a period of retrogression.

Awareness and Understanding of God's Vision for the Church

Leaders in retrogressive congregations talk about the often-painful process of coming to grips with the severity of their situation. The experience common to all retrogressive churches was too many demands on too few resources. What rescued these churches from the ravages of decay was a spiritual reorientation. One pastor expressed it this way. "We got so caught up in all our activity that we were meeting seven days a week. We were buried in papers, planning, proposals. It got so bad that most of our groups dropped devotions from the agenda because we just didn't have the time. Many of us were on the edge of burnout. I took a personal retreat—three days in the woods at a Catholic retreat center—with nothing but a Bible. I read Scripture, I prayed, I meditated, and I walked the woods in silence. I began to feel close to God again, and the thought of going back to the church scared me. I decided then and there that the leadership of the congregation was going to go on retreat—to start things off—then we were going to get serious about praying together, reading the Bible together, meditating, and listening to God. It changed us—turned us around—and we are much better for it, even though it cost us a few warm bodies."

The spiritual refocusing from the top down is the norm in stable congregations. Retrogressive and vital congregational leaders practice the means of grace as a top priority in their ministry together. If the choice comes down to spiritual formation or having a business meeting, spiritual formation wins every time. The commitment to shared spiritual practice guarantees that these congregations include God among their slate of leaders. "We always kind of assumed we included God in our work. I mean, come on, we're the church. It's obvious we're doing all of this for God, right?" One pastor asked. "But it isn't about what we do for God, but what God can do through us. This is God's church, you know? God's plan for God's people. We weren't very good listeners, but we're getting better."

Many churches of all four types talk about the importance of listening to God, but it is in the retrogressive and vital congregations that the strongest evidence of deep, regular listening exists. One of the most spiritually focused, worshipful leadership meetings I ever attended was a Board of Trustees meeting in a suburban retrogressive church. I often think of how fortunate the congregation is that is led by such spiritually mature, focused laity.

Discernment is a key word in retrogressive congregations. The combination of prayer, theological reflection, knowledge of *The Book of Discipline*, critical analysis of human and material resources, and awareness of potential ministries and service result in a clear and compelling vision. While vital congregations often have defining metaphors and stories that reveal their vision, the vision in retrogressive churches tends to be practical, concrete, and unambiguous. The emphasis on God's part in providing a vision is illustrated through a series of random quotes from different churches across the connection:

"We see a need and come together to ask, 'What would God have us do here?'"

"Every week, we begin our time together listing all the things we have done that both honor and glorify God, then in prayer we ask, 'What else would you have us do, Lord?'"

"Every meeting—I mean every meeting—begins with Scripture reading, discussion, a time for prayer, a time for meditation, then a time to talk about what we're thinking. The first forty-five minutes to an hour of our meetings are spent this way, and you know what? Our meetings now are shorter than they used to be and we get more done."

"It is not unusual for us to pray five or six different times each time we meet."

"We don't raise an issue unless we've prayed about it; we don't decide an issue until we've *all* prayed about it."

There are fewer retrogressive congregations than any other type, but leaders in these churches are by far most likely to talk about God's vision for their church. There is a strong correlation between belief that the vision comes from God, and the commitment to the congregation's sense of identity and purpose.

Governing and Guiding Values

The church exists to serve. This, more than any other, emerges as the primary value of retrogressive congregations. If you agree with it, you will most likely be comfortable and find a home in a retrogressive church. However, if comfort, security, being cared for, and being served are your primary values, the retrogressive church will feel very uncomfortable. Retrogressive congregations are "doers of the word, not hearers only." (James 1:22) Participants in these churches more than any of the other three types place the congregation's needs and comfort before their own, and generally place stranger's needs and comfort before their own. One glowing sprite of a woman told me how she was learning to relate to people out on the street. This woman spends most of her free time talking to homeless men and women in shelters. She says, "I would never do this alone, but with my congregation I have the confidence and courage to talk to anybody." When I noted the number of street people who attend worship, Bible study, and fellowship events and how unacceptable they would be in many of our churches, she replied, "We're not supposed to love someone because of the way he smells or dresses or grooms himself, are we? The reason we need to be a church where they can come is because so many others don't want them. That's the thing that has always bugged me about Methodists: We say we want new members, we want more people to come to church, but when we say that we're not talking about these guys, guys who really need us. That kills me. We only really want clean, educated, calm, wealthy Christians. Others need not apply."

As mentioned before, there is often a gulf between our articulated values and our lived values. The gulf between articulated and lived values is most narrow in retrogressive churches. In the seventies vernacular, they "walk the talk."

They also do something shared by most vital congregations: They differentiate the non-negotiables from less important values. There is a clear sense of what is most important, and that is where retrogressive congregations turn their attention. "Okay, we know loving is good, judging is not," explains one Sunday school teacher, "and that healing of any kind beats arguing and divisiveness. We know that forgiveness is way up there, but vengeance is God's so we shouldn't do it. Okay, Mother Teresa and Charles Manson walk into our church. Who belongs here? We figure the best way to answer it is, both of them do, but quite honestly, Manson probably needs love, healing, and forgiveness more than Mother Teresa, so if we were forced to choose just one, it would probably be him.

"We have so few opportunities to do good—to be kind, to heal, to offer grace—we shouldn't waste them by deciding who to condemn, blame, and despise. I personally have a real hard time with homosexuality. I think it's wrong. But when I place it alongside my beliefs about love, grace, acceptance, and the goodness of all creation, it just doesn't matter. In this church, the things we agree on are those important things at the top. The things we disagree about are down lower. We have decided to focus on the top of the list, and ignore the bottom."

This decision to focus on the positive and refusal to be sidetracked by the negative is one healthy and productive way that retrogressive churches avoid conflict, build consensus, and stay focused on their core, defining values.

Impact Awareness

Retrogressive congregations set the gold standard for impact awareness. Leaders of these congregations are clear about what they want to see happen, they do an excellent job mobilizing the community of faith to serve, they know exactly how well or how poorly they have performed, and they figure out how to improve their performance in the future. Because retrogressive congregations tend to focus on the performance of specific ministries to others, it is a simpler task to evaluate effectiveness.

Alongside knowledge of what is having the greatest impact, both on congregational participants as well as the external community, is an honest understanding of where they have the least impact. Leaders in these congregations are as open and honest about what they don't accomplish as what they do. One pastor remarked, "If we had to grade ourselves on a 'God, Neighbor, Self' scale, I think we would be 'B' or 'B+' on God and Neighbor, but probably a 'C-' on Self. That's just not where we are. Ask me, 'Does Dave have a solid prayer life?' and I can't tell you. Ask me 'Does Dave help the poor and needy at least five days a week?' and I can say, 'Absolutely!'" The vast majority of retrogressive congregations (forty-six of the fifty-one churches in the sample) are focused on ministry and service beyond the congregation to the community. In almost every one of these settings, the impact awareness on the community is clearly measured and understood, while the impact awareness of congregational participants is less clearly known. One person surmised, "Well, it's obvious they are growing as Christian disciples because they're here all the time." Spending just a couple days with retrogressive congregations reveals this assumption to be questionable. Many participants are drawn by a passion to one specific thing. When asked if they pray, read the Bible, worship regularly, or engage in theological reflection, they respond in the negative. It is questionable that a holistic, fully integrated Christian discipleship can emerge through a preponderance of acts of mercy to the exclusion of commensurate acts of piety.

Leadership

The shift from unstable congregational types to stable types is the shift from a top-down, pastor-based, representative government form of leadership to a congregation-wide, lay-clergy, integrated form of leadership. The contrast is striking. In more than a few stable congregations, it took me quite some time to figure out who the appointed pastor was, and who were elected leaders. Most retrogressive congregations (due in part to their size) adopt a policy that says, "If the decision will affect your life and faith, then you have a right to participate in the decision making process." This Utopian approach takes more time, but it makes the decision making process virtually transparent. Everyone knows what's going on at all times. The bestowal of authority also confers responsibility, resulting in high levels of ownership and a willingness to step forward in a wide variety of leadership roles.

"Thinking biblically, discipleship equals leadership. If you aren't training people to lead, you are not equipping them to be Christian disciples. It is as simple as that," one pastor remarked. Stable congregations generally see leadership development as a core component of Christian education. Confidence building, critical thinking, and group dynamics are often taught alongside Bible study and technical skill development in stable churches.

A "people skills specialist" from one urban congregation said, "If our ultimate goal is to live our faith in the world as a witness to Christ, we need to lead. Our goal isn't to cultivate leaders for our congregation, but to equip our congregation to lead in the community and world." Once again, this outward focus sees that the purpose of the church is to have a positive impact on the world. People with quality leadership skills will have a greater impact beyond the church walls than those that do not.

Retrogressive congregations are laity-based, laity-led congregations, even in the presence of full-time, appointed pastors. They are so active, that no one individual can adequately manage all the various ministries and programs, not because there are so many, but because each one is so comprehensive. It is important to emphasize that retrogressive congregations are no less active than vital, dystrophic, or decaying congregations (in fact, they tend to be seven-day-a-week churches), but they are active in a few things rather than many. One man used this image: "Let's say we have fifty big construction projects we can bid on. Company A bids on all of them, gets a bunch, and assigns inadequate crews to all of them. Company B selects three jobs it can do better than anybody else and sets a top-flight crew on each one. We're Company B." All workers, fully engaged, all the time, on one or two ministries. Within each ministry, opportunities for specialized focus and service. Making sure that everything runs well all the time in each of the areas—while important work—is not the primary role of the pastor. The role of the pastor is to meet people, guide the community of faith as a whole, and provide the spiritual and theological basis for the congregation's life together. Lay leadership provides all the rest.

As is implied, retrogressive congregations hire very few professional staff. There is a pervasive "if we can't do it ourselves, we won't hire someone else to do it for us" attitude in retrogressive churches. Retrogressive congregations work with professional leaders all the time, but they partner with professionals in the external community. The congregation's sense of identity, purpose, focus, and their defining values go a long way to explain their attitude, which is that God calls a people together to do a great work. There is something fundamentally unacceptable about hiring people to do this work instead.

Smaller churches tend to have fewer paid staff, so it makes sense that retrogressive congregations would have small staffs. But in almost every case (forty-eight of fifty-one churches) the size of the staff was a conscious, strategic decision. "Early on, we realized how deeply disempowering a staff person can be if that person is paid to do something that the congregation ought to do for itself. A good organist or a business administrator may fill a critical need with specialized knowledge no one in the congregation has. That makes sense. But a program coordinator? An evangelism director? I'm sorry, those people need to be nurtured, cultivated, and trained from within. We realized that we had to release almost our whole staff [The pastor served a church with fifteen paid staff positions, including himself. They cut back to two paid positions.] or we could never get healthy again. We studied Gerald May's work on codependency[3] and realized he was talking about us—our congregation's codependent

---

3. Gerald G. May, *Addiction & Grace: Love and Spirituality in the Healing of Addictions* (New York: HarperCollins, 1991).

relationship with staff." It is important to note that retrogressive congregations are not claiming that paid staff are bad, but that critical discernment should be used to determine whether staff perform specialized duties *for* a congregation or *instead* of a congregation.

Retrogressive congregations are very clear about what they want to do, why they want to do it, and what it will take to do it effectively. This includes an analysis of the knowledge, skills, experience, and expertise required. Once necessary leadership skills are assessed, retrogressive congregations engage in a twofold process of skills/gifts discovery, and leadership training and development. Whereas most decaying and dystrophic congregations recruit people to assume leadership roles, vital and retrogressive congregations recruit people to be trained in various leadership roles. This is a huge distinction. Just as Jesus did not immediately thrust the disciples into the forefront of the early movement, stable congregations do not assume that laity leadership is ready to assume full responsibility for ministries within the congregation. There is a great deal of mentoring, team building, and experience building that occurs in stable congregations that is absolutely absent from unstable churches.

The Role of the Appointed Pastor(s)

Many pastors in retrogressive congregations are out on the front lines of the ministry of their churches, but this is never their main function. It is easier to begin by looking at what pastors in retrogressive congregations don't do, to better understand what they do.

Pastors in retrogressive churches do not manage or micro-manage. While capable laity make the day-to-day decisions and conduct the business of the church, pastors remain focused on the guiding vision and values of the congregation. They spend more time looking at where the church needs to move in the future than how it functions in the present (or lament how different things are from the past).

Pastors in retrogressive congregations do not attend a lot of meetings. Trust levels are very high in stable churches. Many of the tactical, decision making meetings in the church require no input from the appointed pastor. What do these pastors do with the five to ten hours freed up when they don't have to sit through unnecessary meetings? The answer is threefold. First, they meet with people to listen and to share the story of the congregation's life. They want to hear where the needs are greatest and where the congregation makes the greatest difference in people's lives. Second, they shepherd other leaders in spiritual reflection and faith formation. These pastors attend to the ongoing spiritual needs of the community of faith, and create those experiences that help leaders grow, develop, and deepen their faith. Third, they spend a large amount of time in prayer, reflection, and discernment, both alone and with others, to attend to God's unfolding vision for the congregation. In these ways, the appointed pastors provide visioning and futuring leadership to the congregation, while relying heavily on qualified lay people to manage the ministry of the church.

Pastors in retrogressive congregations do not pull rank, act autocratically, or overturn decisions made by the elected leaders of the congregation. The image of servant leadership is strong in most retrogressive churches. Since most pastors in effective retrogressive churches understand their primary role as that of equipping and enabling ministry in others, they consciously avoid behaviors that might undermine their efforts.

Being "in charge" is less important than being effective to the pastors of stable congregations. In such a status conscious denomination as United Methodism, many pastors find it challenging to step back and let laity take both the responsibility and credit for work well done. However, the pastors of retrogressive congregations have already made some very hard decisions—decisions that have an impact on membership and attendance in negative ways—so relinquishing credit does little to affect their self-image. It is refreshing to talk with pastors who honestly acknowledge what they don't know and what they look to laypeople for in order to be effective. There is very little "look at how great I am" posturing in retrogressive congregations. The unfortunate side effect of this is that we often do not hear the healthy and powerful story of these ministries, because the pastors don't divert their time to writing books and speaking at conferences.

Perhaps one of the most hopeful and positive aspects of the retrogressive congregation is that their pastors work, on average, about fifty-five hours per week, significantly less than their decaying and dystrophic counterparts. The old cliché, "many hands make light work," seems to explain the phenomena. Repeatedly, I heard from pastors in these congregations statements like, "I don't have to do everything myself." There are exceptions, however. As a category, the pastors of retrogressive congregations attend to personal needs, family needs, spiritual needs, and emotional needs as well as the pastors of vital congregations, but I found a few individual pastors who are champion crusaders for the cause of their congregation, often working twelve-hour days, seven days a week. These individuals are exceptions, and, unbelievably, they seem to thrive on the challenge. But the majority of pastors in retrogressive churches model a very healthy management of workload, family, and self-care.

Programmatic Design

A dramatic difference between stable and unstable congregations can be seen in what these congregations publish in their weekly worship bulletins (or project on their screens). In decaying and dystrophic congregations, everything has a title: "40 Days of Something," "Harvest Festival," "Spring Fling," "Journeys with Jesus," "Handyman's Club." It feels like every study, small group, work project, or meeting is a program of some sort. In vital and retrogressive congregations, few things have titles, unless it reflects a title already bestowed, like, "DISCIPLE Bible Study," "Habitat for Humanity," or, "*Companions in Christ.*" Generally, announcements in retrogressive congregations look like, "Everyone's invited to pack food boxes this Thursday," or "We'll be serving lunches Monday, Wednesday, Friday, and Sunday this week. Helpers appreciated," "Tuesday evening from 7:00 until we're finished we will continue our study of Luke." Reminders are reminders, not marketing.

Leaders in retrogressive (and vital) congregations have broken from the program-based ministry mentality. "Our program is simple—call it the 'Disciples for Life' program—and that is all we do," shared one lay leader. "Everything we offer is an element of that one program. If it helps people live as disciples, we do it; if it doesn't help, we don't do it." This is a common perspective in retrogressive churches.

There is a strong feeling among many leaders of retrogressive congregations that programs can become an excuse not to do ministry. When all of the effort and energy of the congregation goes into creating, designing, promoting, and running a variety of programs, it makes it difficult to assess what is of value and what isn't. The retrogressive approach to ministry is that it is cumulative and developmental; therefore, each experience needs to somehow relate to every other. "Faith formation as a process is very different from faith formation as a program," one Christian education director reflects. "As a process, there is nothing programmatic about it. Oh, a program might help now and then, but a truly integrated, transformative process is more than just a bunch of programs. We have a core of practices and experiences at this church that all work together to build faith, deepen spirituality, and equip people to serve others.

That's just what we do, day after day, week after week. Turning it into a program somehow makes it less important."

The process approach to spiritual development, discipleship, and stewardship defines stable congregations. There are no extraneous programs in these churches—no sewing circles, craft fairs, fundraisers, bake sales, golf outings—only those activities that promote faith development and spiritual formation. Leaders from retrogressive congregations are not against such activities, but feel they are of lesser importance than acts of piety and acts of mercy.

Organizational Structure

"Less is more" is the rule in retrogressive congregations. One congregation drew their organizational chart as one big box with everyone inside. Most churches have not adopted such an extremely simple structure, but many are close to it. Basically, the structure of a retrogressive congregation is flat, lean, and remarkably effective. One representative structure mimicked by many other retrogressive congregations is an oversight committee of five to seven members with representative chairs of ministry, personnel, administrative, and financial focus areas.

In this simplified structure, every major need of the congregation can be adequately met, while freeing leadership within each area to stay focused. Additionally, in this model the top tier is charged to attend to the visioning/futuring concerns, while the second tier focuses on the futuring/managing functions. Both levels intentionally receive input from the whole participating congregation. The specifics may look different from congregation to congregation, but the four general areas are very consistent.

How does it work? Leaders in retrogressive churches report a higher level of satisfaction with the way things run than leaders in the other three church types. The combination of clear focus, deep commitment, shared responsibility, good communication (communication is much easier in a flat, simple structure), and congregation-wide support makes the experience of leading especially enjoyable. No retrogressive congregation reported any difficulty in handling decisions, workload, or implementation with a simplified structure.

Three congregations developed "evaluations teams" separate from every other team. The purpose of such a team is not to make sure teams and work areas do their work, but to partner with each working group to evaluate how well they are doing. The three congregations all report significant value added to their ministries by such groups. More will be discussed about evaluation teams in the chapter on vital congregations.[4]

In a significant majority of the retrogressive churches (thirty-five of fifty-one) the pastor attends only the oversight group meeting, and second tier meetings by invitation. For most pastors in this category, the message is clear: ministry does not equal meetings. A number of pastors reported that this was a serious struggle, either for them personally or for their congregations. Some pastors have a hard time believing that their sparkling and incisive insights aren't essential to the effectiveness of a meeting. Many congregational leaders believe the pastor's voice is necessary for any decision a church makes. Sometimes, district superintendents and conference leaders assume and/or expect pastors to attend all church meetings. Climbing out from under the toxic misconception that pastors need to be in meetings is one of the stiffest challenges that many pastors face. However, reports from these retrogressive churches indicate that everyone, including the pastor, works more effectively when fewer meeting demands are placed on the pastoral leader.

Money

Money is funny. Churches that need the most seem never to have enough, while those that have a lot seem to have no trouble getting more. Retrogressive congregations are some of the most financially sound churches in the United Methodist denomination. This is counter-intuitive, since they are experiencing a decline in membership and attendance; it makes sense that they would suffer a commensurate loss of funding. However, the people who choose to leave retrogressive congregations tend not to be the best or biggest givers. Those who remain tend to deepen their involvement, and their investment as well. Leaders in local congregations tend to be the best givers. When a church broadens its leadership base—widening the circle of decision makers, innovators, and those authorized to make things happen—it automatically improves the giving level of those new leaders. Almost three-quarters of the participants in retrogressive congregations give in the top giving tier. (See appendix 3) It is not uncommon for leaders in these churches to be giving 14%, 17%, or 20% of their income (yes,

---

4. Evaluation teams are novel in retrogressive churches, non-existent in decaying and dystrophic congregations, while fairly common in vital churches. There is a strong correlation between vitality and sound critical evaluation.

gross—not net) to the ministries and work of the congregation. This reflects the power of aligning the missional focus of a congregation with the gifts, passions, values, and sense of call of individual men and women.

No retrogressive congregation in the study employs an annual giving campaign. One reason is that they don't think or act programmatically, and most stewardship campaigns are designed and delivered as programs. More importantly, they don't use campaigns because they don't need to. When giving is an integral part of the definition and description of faithful Christian stewards and disciples, there is little need to talk people into doing what they should already be doing. The need for campaigns is a fairly clear sign of decay (decline of funds, unsustainable ministry), and this is not true of retrogressive churches. Sampling nine retrogressive congregations, the average annual giving of new members is $4,271 a year.[5]

Retrogressive congregations have the money they need to do ministry for one other simple, but significant reason: they ask for it. Beyond giving within the congregation, retrogressive congregations cultivate financial support from members of the community, other agencies, and other churches—anything that helps them effectively minister to people's needs. Leaders in retrogressive congregations solicit the donation of property, equipment, food, clothing, professional services, building and medical supplies. Money, so often a taboo subject in unstable congregations, is non-controversial in retrogressive churches. One laywoman summed it up, "I say, 'We need money. Will you give?' and you respond either 'yes' or 'no,' and either one is fine with me. So, what's the big deal?" What is remarkable are the number of people who say "yes" to retrogressive church requests.

The Role of Worship in the Life of the Congregation

Retrogressive congregations have an interesting relationship with worship. Worship services—so central to the life of dystrophic and decaying congrega-

5. Average annual giving of new members in the other three congregational types: Vital, $2,441; Dystrophic, $1,487, Decaying $1,156. Dystrophic congregations receive the most members from higher educational and economic demographics. Vital and retrogressive congregations pull in the highest percentage of newcomers living below the poverty line. High numbers of inactive newcomers skew dystrophic and decaying figures downward; high numbers of low income members skew vital and retrogressive figures downward.

tions—are peripheral to the ministry of retrogressive congregations. Services are held on Sunday, a few offered through the week, but worship is of lesser importance to leaders of retrogressive congregations than active participation in service, outreach, or small groups. Some retrogressive churches have actually moved their worship from Sunday morning to be available to serve hot meals to the hungry, to do hospital visitation, or to have Bible study with a larger number of people.

Worship is less a whole congregation affair, and more of an intimate experience. Small groups worship together. Work teams worship together. Leadership teams worship together. Worship is less about making sure everyone is together in one place doing the same thing, and more about making sure that covenant groups make sure they focus on God on a regular basis.

"Worship isn't about us," one young man told me. "It doesn't happen for just one hour the same time every week. Worship is the honest expression of gratitude and admiration for God, and it can happen at any time in any place. I worship more since I joined this church than I ever have in my life, but I haven't been to Sunday morning services in almost a year." Another person in another church clear across the country shared the sentiment. "Worship isn't just something we do. It sure isn't something we 'attend.' Worship is part of what makes us who we are. You can't can it and march it out once a week and make it meaningful. My DISCIPLE group meets on Tuesdays before work and we worship together. My Habitat group still meets once a month and we worship. Both of those experiences mean so much more than any Sunday service I can recall."

Not everyone is comfortable with this more fluid approach to worship. When I share my findings with large groups, invariably someone will mutter in disgust, "That's not worship." There is still a very strong sense in the United States that authentic Christian worship takes place when everyone gathers together in a church sanctuary on Sunday morning. Forget that this is essentially a modern phenomenon with no biblical basis; it has become orthodoxy to the vast majority of decaying and dystrophic churches, and to a large majority of American churchgoers.

Worship is very important to participants of retrogressive fellowships, but not Sunday services. It is never a choice between worship or staying in bed for participants in retrogressive congregations; it is a choice of when to worship and when to serve or learn or lead.

The Role of Education in the Life of the Congregation

Learning in retrogressive congregations focuses on the concrete over the conceptual or abstract. Bible study is to understand God's will for the church and to learn how to live the Christian life. Sunday school classes focus on the priorities of the congregation and deepen the knowledge of what the church can do to make a difference. Specialized learning opportunities teach people skills to use in ministry to others. One happy retired man asked me, "Why waste time teaching people to think theologically when you can teach them how to use a band saw?"

Among laity in retrogressive congregations there is strong sentiment that much that passes for Christian education in the church impedes spiritual growth and formation, instead of promoting it. When Scripture is approached as theoretical and abstract, people can discuss and debate it endlessly, and not do much with it. This is unacceptable in retrogressive churches. It is one thing to sit in a comfortable room discussing the positive and negatives of "take up your cross daily and follow me," (Luke 9:23) and another to actually do it. Retrogressive churches teach people how to carry their cross.

Most participants in retrogressive congregations do not "belong" to a particular Sunday school class, but they attend whatever classes help them progress to the next level in their faith development. If they cannot find what they are looking for in their own church, they may seek it out in another church or in the community. There is an honest awareness that a single church cannot possibly teach everything every person needs to know to grow in the Christian faith. Therefore, education is process rather than program. Learning is central to the growth of every Christian disciple, but the church's role is not so much to do the teaching as it is to help guide each disciple on their ongoing journey. One church developed a series of internships with various companies throughout the community to help equip people for missionary service. Another church works with a community college to allow church participants to audit classes. This "out-of-the-box" thinking is not unusual in stable congregations.

The Congregation's Relationship to the Community

In virtually every retrogressive context, the relationship of the congregation to the community is strong and vital. Church isn't the building in which the congregation gathers, it is the gathered body dispersed back into the world. Church only becomes real when it becomes active, and the primary center of its activity is the world.

Retrogressive congregations build networks with other churches, civic organizations, community services, and businesses to maximize the positive impact of their ministries. It is not unusual to find retrogressive congregations hosting and directing ecumenical ministries.

Often, the pastors of large congregations are well known throughout their community. In the case of retrogressive congregations, both clergy and laity are well known for their ministries and service to the community. Where decaying and dystrophic congregations spend the majority of their efforts attempting to get people to come to them, retrogressive and vital congregations spend the majority of their time reaching out to connect with people where they are. Location (such a high priority in our church growth mania culture) is of little importance to retrogressive congregations. If a church is mobilized to move into the community to meet needs and be in ministry, it doesn't much matter what the building looks like. As one pastor expressed it, "God certainly doesn't need pretty windows, big statues, the latest and greatest technology, and a big parking lot, and they can't feed the hungry or care for the sick. No way you can justify all that stuff and call yourself a Christian church.

The Congregation's Relationship to the Connectional System

There is no diplomatic way to describe the relationship of most retrogressive congregations to the connectional system: it's bad. And where it isn't bad, it's worse. There are one or two exceptions, but a number of factors contribute to a poor relationship between the annual conference and a retrogressive congregation.

First, retrogressive churches are losing members and show declining worship attendance in the short-term. Fewer pew-occupiers are anathema in our denomination. A mere twelve disciples by our reckoning is a bona-fide failure. Jesus obviously hasn't read the latest publications of our premiere pastors who draw people in by the hundreds, if not thousands. The leaders of retrogressive churches deeply resent the fact that most connectional and conference leaders continue to measure inputs instead of outputs. Fifty people feeding one thousand hot meals a week is nowhere valued as highly as five hundred people feeding no one.

Second, retrogressive congregations are flagged as "problems'" in almost every one of our annual conferences. A pastor who holds people accountable to their membership vows and expects church participants to balance acts of mercy with acts of piety is difficult to appoint to a church of low standards and low expectations. Conversely, a congregation motivated to live their faith as vital stewards and disciples will no longer tolerate a pastor who wants to create a safe, comfortable, inert enclave. A second-career pastor confided to me, "My District Superintendent told me I had to stop doing what I'm doing here because I am causing a blockage in the appointment system. Nobody wants to come here, and no other church wants me as their pastor. Can you believe that?"

Third, participants in retrogressive congregations avoid serving on district and conference committees. Leaders who have struggled to do away with unnecessary and dysfunctional systems and processes in their own congregations are not likely to want to engage in them at the conference level. This "unwillingness" to serve is viewed as uncooperative by conference leaders who desperately want to employ gifted, talented, and experienced leaders from these congregations. Speaking with conference leaders, some of the retrogressive congregations are viewed as "standoffish" or as thinking they are "better than the rest of us." Having visited these churches, I did not encounter any feelings of superiority or overt actions taken to distance the congregation from the conference. I did, however, get a distinct impression that retrogressive churches are square pegs at odds with the round holes the conference wishes they would fit into.

Summarizing the Retrogressive Condition

Retrogressive churches have little drawing appeal to a wide audience. They are a perfect fit for a select group of people who share similar passions, desires, and vision for ministry. They are powerfully effective at what they do, though they tend to be fairly small in number.

A narrow focus is essential to allow these churches to become stable, and to position themselves for expansion and growth. Holding too narrow a focus for too long undermines the stabilizing factors, damages the overall health of the congregation, and leads to decay.

Generally, the congregation finds its sense of identity, purpose, and vision in a single ministry, or maybe two ministries. For nine out of ten retrogressive churches, the ministry is one of outreach and witness. In many cases, an integrated process of spiritual formation and development of the community of faith do not balance this outward focus. Balancing acts of piety with acts of mercy is critically important to move retrogressive congregations toward vitality.

We can learn a lot from retrogressive congregations about collaborative ministries and networking. A limitation in the congregation's resources never limits the vision of a retrogressive church. If the need is out there and it aligns with the congregation's values, vision, and sense of purpose and identity, then a retrogressive church will partner with anyone and everyone to get the job done.

Retrogression is a healthy next step for decaying congregations or for dystrophic congregations on the verge of decline. The crucial work of simplifying, prioritizing, and focusing are powerful stabilizing forces. Establishing membership standards and accountability, flattening the organizational hierarchy and sharing leadership, and developing awareness of impact also move a congregation toward greater stability and health. Retrogressive congregations stand at a critical threshold: If they broaden their base and balance their inward and outward focus, they lay a solid foundation for vitality, but if they fail to attract new participants they will surely slide toward decay.

CHAPTER FOUR

The Vital Congregation

You know you're in a vital church the moment you step through the door; there's just something in the air. Everything about them gives you confidence that they are in a good place. They are not perfect. I want to repeat that: Vital churches are not perfect. But they are moving on to perfection in the best Wesleyan sense.

It is not far wrong to say that vital churches blend the very best aspects of retrogressive and dystrophic churches, dispensing with their flaws and limitations. The big difference between retrogressive and vital churches is the seamless balance of acts of piety and acts of mercy—a fertile and vibrant inner life combined with an exhilarating outreach and Christian witness. A teenager in one of the vital congregations suggested this incredible image for the balance of acts of mercy and piety; "It's like breathing. Acts of piety are inhaling; acts of mercy are exhaling. They go together. People may ask, which is most important, but the answer is, 'It depends on which you did last.' Life [vitality] depends on an equal measure of both."

The greatest difference between vital and dystrophic churches is the way they view growth. Dystrophic churches devote an enormous amount of energy to getting bigger; growth is a goal and an end in itself. In vital churches, growth is a byproduct of healthy practices. Just as muscle develops through rigorous exercise, so a vital church grows through the faithful practice of spiritual disciplines. Where a congregation realizes its potential as the body of Christ, it is extremely attractive to outsiders. Vital congregations find that they have no trouble drawing and keeping new participants, though their numeric increases may not be as dramatic as most of their dystrophic counterparts.

One of the questions I am most frequently asked about vital churches is, "Why don't we hear more about them?" I don't fully understand this myself, but I suspect that the answer is twofold. First, vital churches focus on ministry, not self-promotion. Pastors in these churches don't write books, and leaders in these congregations do not present their story as a model to emulate. Each vital congregation worked a long, intentional, thorough process of self-discovery unique to its context. Vital congregations do not offer a simple formula for other churches to copy.

Second, vital congregations establish rigorous standards for member-ship and participation. It is not easy to lead or participate in a vital church. Vital churches are hard work, and many American Christians have little interest in pursuing a demanding faith. Vital congregations take disciple-ship and stewardship seriously—something most churches merely pay lip service to. Just as the human body requires a proper diet, regular exercise, and renewing activity such as sleep and purposeful work, vital churches require solid spiritual food, regular practice of spiritual disciplines, and renewing activities such as Sabbath rest, worship, and contemplative study. Vitality comes through scrupulous discipline, which many Christians would rather do without.

Vital churches experience the transforming power of God's Spirit in indi-vidual lives, and in both the internal and external community. Leaders in these congregations devote themselves to cultivating and nurturing an environment where everyone is able to experience God's presence and power. Very little hap-pens in vital churches that is not a part of an intentional, comprehensive, and strategic design to build and strengthen the body of Christ.

Vital congregations demand the very highest levels of sacrifice and com-mitment, but in every case the benefits far outweigh the costs. Participants in these churches are energized, motivated, excited, and engaged. Church is not simply a part of their lives—they *are* the church twenty-four hours a day, seven days a week, three hundred sixty-five days a year (and the extra day each leap year as well).

Sense of Identity

We. "We" is the word spoken most frequently in vital congregations. The community of faith comes first. It is striking to be in a large group of people where individual agendas are set aside for the common good, but that is the norm in vital churches. Unity, connection, oneness, and communion are defining terms for these congregations. This is not to say there is no disagreement or conflict in these churches, but where disagreement exists, there is a healthy, respectful way to address it. No individual ever imposes his or her will on the community of faith. It simply isn't allowed. Vital congregations are striking for the absence of "toxic influencers." Bad behavior is confronted, challenged, and either fixed or removed. Such is the importance of modeling Christian unity and grace.

The guiding metaphor for vital churches is the body of Christ. This organic model expresses wonderfully what vital congregations strive to achieve: one healthy, vibrant, magnificent incarnation of Jesus Christ for the world. Vital churches value anything that builds the body; while those things that hurt the body are avoided.

Decaying and dystrophic churches tend to describe themselves in terms of the programs they provide, but vital churches speak much more foundationally about beliefs, values, and vision. Members of vital churches talk less about what their churches "do" and more about what they experience there. The church is a place to encounter God, to grow in faith and faithfulness, to discern God's will, to build community, and to develop the gifts and graces from God. Invitations are to journey with the congregation, to participate in the discernment of God's will, and to seek meaning and purpose in an open, honest, and safe environment—not to attend worship or join a group. There is a gentle and respectful "come and see" offered by these churches: come and see if there isn't a place for you here, come and see if God will not knit and weave you into the fabric of this community, come and see what God might have in store for us both.

The sense of identity in vital churches is ultimately this: We are who we are. We are a community gifted by God, called by God, inspired by God, and loved by God. We are the body of Christ, faithfully striving to be one in mind, heart, and spirit. We are not a building, club, place, or organization. We are the church, and we would love it if this is the place both you and God want you to be.

Shared Clarity of Purpose

Vital churches keep purpose and mission clearly and cleanly separated. Few vital congregations argue with the denominational mission, "to make disciples of Jesus Christ,"[1] but no vital church is satisfied to let it end there. Discipleship is a means to an end for vital churches. Vital churches are kingdom builders (for want of a better, less patriarchal phrase) doing all they can to spread scriptural holiness across the land and become the body of Christ through which God transforms the world. Effectively fulfilling the mission of the denomination enables a vital church to fulfill its own congregational purpose. For example, one church described the relationship this way: "We make disciples to preach, to teach, and to heal that everyone we meet may know the love of God and the goodness of Christ through us. We exist that people might know the love of God and the goodness of Christ—this is our purpose. Our purpose depends on our ability to effectively fulfill the mission of The United Methodist Church."

A lay leader of a second congregation explains it this way. "Our purpose is to heal the world—or at least be a source of healing, a healing influence—on whatever part of the world we encounter. God's world is broken in so many ways, and God's people are broken in so many ways. We're here to bring God's grace and healing power to all the brokenness. Making disciples, helping people live their faith in the world, is the best way we can lay that foundation for healing."

Vital churches develop short, simple ways to describe their purpose to others. Purpose emerges from the shared journey of faith of the congregational body, not from a committee developing a mission statement. Talk to anyone in a vital church and they will be able to explain the purpose of the congregation. Even visitors to these churches can tell you what the church is all about, the sense of purpose is so ubiquitous.

The purpose of vital churches is more than an ideal—it is an orientation toward the world. "Church is a verb, rather than a noun, here," shares a thirty-something surgeon from the Midwest. "No one simply comes here to receive—though you do receive a lot. It is very clear that this church exists to make a difference in the world, and if you come through the door, it is your job to help it make a difference."

Her husband picks up the thread, and moves in a different direction. "For

1. *The Book of Discipline*.

me, church was always a spectator sport, you know, like football. My role was to be an armchair quarterback. Here, there are no stands; there are no fans. You're either in the game, on the field, or you're nowhere. Lots of people come here, see what is expected of them, and turn around saying, 'You people are crazy. I'm going down the street where I can slip in the pew and nobody will ask me to do anything.' But some people come here, are amazed at how challenging it is, and they say, 'This is what I've always wanted.' Those are the people we want here."

A strong clarity of purpose helps newcomers understand exactly what it means to be a member of the community of faith. It helps people know whether or not they will fit in. It gives people something concrete to measure against. "It 'raises the bar,' if you will, but it sends a clear message: 'This is what it means to be a Christian disciple.' People can take it or leave it, but they know exactly what it is they're getting into," explains the chair of the trustees of one vital church. "We exist for a reason, and the only way we can be effective is if every single person is active and on board."

Focus of the Congregation

Vital congregations describe their focus in a number of ways, but the essence of all they say is this: We want to be Christ incarnate for the world and all of God's people. This focus requires vital churches to balance and integrate a solid inward and outward focus. There is a sense of rhythm to the life of the vital church—a constant flow into the community of faith and out into the world. One high school music teacher explains it this way, "We gather here to rehearse, we leave here to perform. Each performance reveals our limitations and where we need to improve. Each rehearsal helps us overcome our limitations and strengthen our proficiencies. There is no end to the process. No one ever arrives or achieves absolute perfection, but we continuously strive for the next level."

This striving to improve—both the personal and shared spiritual journey and the witness and service to the community and world—is a chief character-istic of the vital church. There is an intentional developmental structure built into vital congregations. Vital congregations acknowledge that some Christians are just embarking on their relationship with God, some have made an early commitment to Christian discipleship, some are quickly maturing in their life of faith, some have been deeply transformed by the Spirit and are leading in signif-icant ways, while others are powerful masters and teachers, apostles, and saints. Vital churches create environments appropriate to all levels of Christian development, empowering and enabling Christians at all levels to grow in the inward and outward expressions of their faith. In one setting, the deeply rooted, spiritually centered members of the congregation meet for an intensely contemplative worship early on Sunday morning, then they lead worship for the segment of the congregation actively pursuing Christian discipleship, who in turn lead a third worship service for newcomers and novices in the Christian faith. Participants self-select the experience most suitable for them in their journey of faith, but at each level leaders farther along in their formation mentor and nurture those who follow. This structure builds in the natural rhythm of receiving and giving, breathing in the spiritual nourishment, breathing out nourishment for others. Focus inward to grow in faith, focus outward to grow faith in others.

This rhythmic focus is evident almost exclusively in vital congregations. Often dystrophic, retrogressive, and decaying churches espouse putting faith into action, but it is an option, a suggestion, and congregational leaders are not always clear on how well people integrate what they hear in church to the way they live their lives through the week. This ambiguity does not exist in vital churches.

Awareness and Understanding of God's Vision for the Church

Vital churches are churches at prayer. And it is the life of prayer that once more makes vital congregations unique. Vital church participants are convinced that God is continually speaking, and that it is essential that God's people take time to listen. Members of vital churches pray, talk about prayer, study prayer, think about prayer, and teach prayer. Vital churches have reclaimed prayer as a core practice of the church. Individuals are taught to pray, reminded to pray, encouraged to pray, and held accountable for prayer. Many times, leaders in these churches come together for no other purpose than to pray.

It is from this deep, rich life of prayer that the identity, clarity of purpose, focus, and vision of the vital church emerges. Prayer in the vital church is an equal measure of speaking and listening to God. Silence, a foreign and strange (and often uncomfortable) experience in decaying, dystrophic, and retrogressive churches, is a normal experience in vital churches. Members are encouraged to listen, to quiet themselves, to attend to their hearts and souls, and to share what they find there.

Because prayer is so omnipresent, and the encouragement to share the prayer experience so common, vision—especially vision from God—is a regular part of the conversation. "We are constantly discussing God's will, here," one pastor remarks. "I confess that my prayer life has been sporadic throughout my ministry, but not here. This congregation has ministered to me in so many ways—reminds me daily of why I wanted to be a pastor. In a very kind and loving way, the leaders of this church said to me, 'You know, we are interested in what you have to say to us, but we're more interested in what God has to say to us.' It has taught me that I'm not the only one who knows what God might want for the church. God is speaking to many people—people who listen much better than I."

This comment reveals another important lesson from the vital church—God reveals God's vision through many hearts, minds, and voices, not just the pastor's. Many decaying and dystrophic congregations hold a misguided view that the pastor is the most appropriate visionary leader of a congregation. And while it is true that a pastor holds a unique position from which to lift up and hold forth a vision, in no way is a pastor more likely to receive a vision from God. Given the sorry state of the prayer life of most ordained clergy, it is highly unlikely that many are even paying attention to God's vision. In vital churches, the vision comes to a variety of leaders, and it is tested and perfected in the hearts of the community, not just a few individuals. "Moses didn't receive the vision because he was the leader," reminds one jolly matriarch of a small vital church. "He became a powerful leader because he received the vision. Our church is growing, not because our pastor said, 'This is God's vision given to me for you.' Our pastor is helping us grow because he says, 'You have helped me see God's vision for this church and I have these gifts to support and pursue it.'" Vital churches are stable and sustainable because the vision belongs to the congregation, not to the pastor. There is no need to "sell" a vision, or to get people "on board." Vision emerges through the life of the congregation, saturating and infusing the whole community of faith (including the pastoral leadership).

Governing and Guiding Values

There are three central values evident in the life of vital congregations:

1. the community of faith is more important than any individual

2. the community and world is more important than the community of faith

3. becoming one in Christ is the way we honor and glorify God

To be like Christ in all ways is the driving force in vital churches. Many vital churches lift up Romans 12 and Philippians 2:1-13 as defining Scriptures that define for them what it means to be "church."

As with retrogressive congregations, vital churches coalesce around the most important values shared in common, and they refuse to be divided by lesser values. In every vital church, wide agreement around two or three defining values is evident. Vital congregations are grounded in loving, healing, mending, reconciling, mercy, grace, justice, and acceptance. They reject judgment, division, pettiness, hostility, resentment, and dishonesty in all forms. They do not reject anger and disagreement, but develop healthy and respectful ways of dealing with legitimate differences of opinion. Conflict is not seen as a bad thing, but as opportunity to learn and grow, and pain is seen as a clear sign that something needs healing. Communication is highly valued, and the workings of the congregation are open and transparent. Every opinion is respected and regarded, but ultimately it is the consensus of the whole community that prevails. People in vital churches speak passionately, disagree freely, courageously defend their opinions, and maturely abide by the decisions made by the community—even when they are diametrically opposed to their own. Our denomination sorely needs to learn and develop such healthy skills if we are to live up to the "united" prominently displayed in our name.

A crystal clear sense of identity, understanding of purpose, focus, and vision, grounded in the highest shared values result in a community sharing one heart, one mind, and one spirit— proclaiming faith with one accord. There is no room for disgruntled individuals to harm the life of the congregation. Toxic influencers[2] are not tolerated. Bad behavior is named and rejected. Conflict is addressed, passive-aggressive behavior challenged, and gossip refused. These remarkable facts reflect how strongly values inform conduct in vital churches. More than any other church types, vital churches have bridged the chasm between articulated and lived values. What vital congregations say they believe and how they live are one and the same.

I want to be clear here. Vital churches are not perfect. They have problems. But what they also have are healthy, clear, well-designed ways to deal with their problems. Vital congregations are proactive, rather than reactive, and they do not ignore situations that could harm the congregation's life together. This willingness to confront the messy and difficult circumstances is rare. It is one more quality that sets vital churches apart.

2. See note 5 in ch. 1.

Impact Awareness

Because vital congregations are continuously communicating, vital churches are deeply aware of the impact their ministries have on people's lives. Impact awareness, more than any other criteria, distinguishes stable from unstable churches. How people's behaviors change, how they develop their faith and understanding of their relationship with God, how their faith adds value to the community and world, and where they are in their lifelong journey toward God—these are measures by which vital churches assess their effectiveness. If the goal of the church is to become Christ for the world, then two key metrics must be in place: in what ways are we like Christ? and in what ways is the world better off for our existence? These things cannot be measured by attendance figures or giving numbers. The only way to assess impact is to measure the outputs—what has improved, how has it improved, and what value has been added?

Vital churches do a wonderful job integrating qualitative measures with quantitative measures. A Lay Leader (and professional Sociologist) explains it this way: "It is important to reach new people, to grow numerically, but that is never enough. Your goal can never be 'x number of people.' 'Warm bodies' isn't enough. You need a vision for each warm body. There is a big difference between 'a Christian believer' and 'a Christian disciple' and 'a member of Christ's body.' Each one is a matter of degree. One says, 'I think Christ is a great guy,' another says, 'I am willing to make sacrifices to follow Christ,' and the last says, 'I want to be Christlike in every way.' Okay, the way you measure each one is different. In the church, we tend to count only the first type, because it's easiest. A person shows up in church, it's a good bet they like Jesus. But just showing up doesn't tell you whether that person is following Jesus, is growing as a disciple. To understand that you have to establish a set of criteria by which you define 'disciple.' Same thing is true only more so when you want to evaluate how much a person resembles Christ in thought, word, and deed. Each level builds off the quantitative to a greater level of qualitative complexity." Vital churches plumb the depths of qualitative complexity.

This is done through a wide variety of relational experiences—small groups, classes, studies, mentoring, counseling, and spiritual direction—all based in developmental goal setting and accountability. Vital congregations work with individuals to develop comprehensive and detailed spiritual formation plans, and design processes to enable members of the community of faith to achieve their developmental goals. More will be said in the section on the role of education, but one feature prominent in many vital churches is that people can describe how they are planning to grow in their faith—what books they will read, what people they will talk to, and what classes and groups they will participate in that will help them deepen their faith and help them grow in relationship with God. This reflects both the congregational commitment to becoming the body of Christ and the sense of responsibility that members of these churches feel for each other.

Externally, vital churches are every bit as clear on the impact their shared life together has on the community and world. The community is also aware of the congregation's impact. Residents of the community in which a vital church is located share endless stories of the way they personally have been served by the church, as well as stories of the many ways others benefit as well. These stories go well beyond a list of programs and services the church offers. These are stories of ways the church touches and saves lives, rescues the perishing, intervenes in crisis situations, raises the community's morale, and in some cases standard of living. Vital churches give life, and they shine as a beacon of hope and grace in their communities.

Leadership

As in retrogressive congregations, vital churches equate authentic Christian living with leading. Every person is gifted; therefore every person contributes to the leadership of community in Christ. The body of Christ is the vessel through which the healing work of Christ continues in the world. A healthy body requires every part to work together with the other parts. Vital congregations dedicate themselves to enabling and equipping each person to understand, develop, and employ his or her gifts for ministry. Beyond that, vital congregations create environments where people can learn skills, gain knowledge and experience, and strengthen leadership abilities.

Vital congregations eliminate the category of inactive members from the fellowship. Membership in a vital church requires active participation in the life of the faith community, and living the faith daily in the world. Membership is not measured in worship attendance or monetary giving. Membership is measured in terms of worldview and lifestyle, beliefs and behaviors, lived out as participants in the body of Christ. "Members are here. If you aren't here, you aren't a member. We let people know that the church is always here for them—we will care for them, visit them, greet them when they visit—but if they want to be a member, then they will work with us, meet with us, pray with us, worship with us, laugh and cry with us on pretty much a daily basis. We aren't a social club; there are no dues, and we don't just meet once a week. It isn't optional whether you participate or not. Churches have gotten sloppy, and membership has become meaningless. Why bother joining if it doesn't matter whether you show up or not? I came from a church with 40% of the members inactive. I ask you, how healthy is a body where 40% doesn't function anymore? It's sick, so to be healthy you need to excise the dead flesh. We have standards. [3] We tell people what it means to be a member here. Take it or leave it. Jesus had standards, we have standards. People are shocked when they find out we expect them to actually do something; they think the church is here just to serve them. That's not the church. The church isn't where you go to be served, where you go is supposed to help you learn to *be* the church." This is a composite statement of many quotes from participants in vital congregations. They point out that in vital churches there aren't leaders and followers. In vital churches, all who follow Jesus Christ are leaders, no exceptions.

Vital congregations generally have well designed processes for leadership cultivation, development, training, and support. Mentoring is widespread, where existing leaders shepherd the next generation of leaders. Rather than following a prescribed definition of what a "good" leader looks like, vital congregations help individuals discover their strengths, gifts, and passions, then link them with the best opportunities for service.

As with everything else in vital churches, leadership is a collaborative, shared process. Vital churches do not emphasize effective leaders, but effective leadership. There are leaders in functional roles in the church (those responsible for making decisions and overseeing the whole organization), but they serve primarily as facilitators and guides. Vital congregations do the best job of differentiating and integrating the three spheres of effective leadership: visioning,

---

3. Holding people accountable to membership standards is the most controversial and frequently challenged aspect of my research. Many leaders (laity, clergy, conference, and episcopal) claim that we "have no right" to impose stringent standards on those who attend church, and that it will only result in fewer members. It has been said that telling a person he or she can't be a member of a church is somehow un-Christian (unless of course they are doing something we find repugnant; then we can deny them) and that we violate our mission if we make discipleship difficult. However, there is overwhelming evidence that the absence of clear, measurable, enforceable membership standards leads to a church defined by its lowest common denominator: the church shopper/Christian consumer.

futuring, and management. By consensus, people are placed in the sphere or spheres where their particular gifts and abilities will do the most good for the most people.

Vital churches depend very little on paid staff. They don't need much staff because they design their ministry and focus around the gifts, skills, passions, and vision of the congregation. Vital churches live from their identity and purpose, therefore they don't need paid professionals to do their ministry for them. The correlation is very strong—the more stable a congregation is, the fewer paid staff it employs; the less stable a congregation is, the more paid staff it employs.

Something that leaders of vital churches do better than leaders of any other type is deal with change. Resistance to change is evident in all four church types, but the community culture in vital churches makes the navigation of change incredibly elegant. Change is not feared, fought, or forbidden in vital churches. The question is rarely, "Will we change," but rather, "How will we change?" Every change poses new opportunities and possibilities for vital churches. Leaders in these churches are aware that their current health and vitality are the direct result of key changes. Vital churches guard against complacency and regard change as a dynamic for renewal and regeneration. Leaders in vital congregations are cognizant of the nature of change, the dynamics of change, and the responses to change. They are extremely effective at leading the congregation through change.

One last observation may be made of leaders in vital churches: They understand human beings and group dynamics. Grace abounds in vital congregations. A significant reason that conflict occurs less frequently in vital churches is that people are allowed to be people—flawed, fallen, imperfect, but loved. How people think, speak, withhold, react, process information, and make decisions are well understood and respected. Leaders in vital churches understand not only *what* happens when people get together, but they understand *why* it happens. The ability to help the community understand the dynamics of group process is a skill in evidence in stable, growing congregations.

The Role of the Appointed Pastor(s)

The description of the role of the appointed/assigned pastor in a vital church is very similar to that of the retrogressive church. The primary role is one of spiritual guide and resident theologian. The pastor aligns the spiritual focus and the vision for ministry and continuously holds this relationship before the congregation. "Our pastor reminds us of who we are every time we are together. That is his most important function," states one Church Council chairperson. "We want him to share his knowledge and understanding of Scripture and theology and challenge us to wrestle with the most challenging questions of our faith." Though the metaphor doesn't hold the power it once did, the primary role of the pastor in a vital church is a shepherding role.

"The grace is, I don't have to be in charge," shares one pastor. "The weight of the world isn't on my back. Christ is the head of this body, and I am one blessed and privileged part. I am allowed to use my gifts here, and this family of wonderful people use theirs to do the things I am not called or gifted to do. Together, we are greater than the sum of our parts. I am a much better pastor because I am no longer trying to do it all." This is a common sentiment of pastors in vital churches.

"I have never been in a church like this before," comments one pastor. "They [other leaders] turn to me for my opinion on relevant matters, but generally they don't need me at all. They honor my teaching and counseling abilities, put up with my on-again, off-again preaching, but they never expect me to do the things I'm no good at."

"I can preach here," another pastor marveled. "Not only do they allow it, but they expect that I will spend hours working on my sermons and Bible study lessons. They don't want me wasting time running around or attending meetings. The chair of my Pastor Parish Committee sat me down and said, 'Look, you are a wonderful preacher and teacher. This congregation benefits most when you teach and preach. Focus on that, and let us worry about the rest.' I had to walk outside and check the sign. I can hardly believe this is a United Methodist church. In my last church, I was expected to set up chairs and tables for church suppers. Here I'm expected to actually proclaim the word of God!"

The gifts, skills, knowledge, and abilities of the appointed pastor are honored and exploited (in the positive sense of the word) in vital churches. They find that they do less, and have a greater impact on people's lives. Rarely do the pastors in vital churches work more than fifty to sixty hours per week, but they spend a much greater percentage of their time engaged in ministries they enjoy and for which they are truly gifted.

Pastors in vital churches find they spend very little time in meetings. "Meetings are the great time waster in the church," one pastor proclaimed. "My entire sense of meaningful work was tied up in meetings before. It felt like I wasn't doing my job if I wasn't running from meeting to meeting. Once I wised up, I realized that meetings weren't ministry, they *replaced* ministry. In this church, we turned it around. We replace meetings with ministry." This is not to say that meetings do not have their place, and that churches can get by with no meetings, but in vital churches meetings serve a strategic purpose, and they are tightly focused and highly efficient. "We meet for an hour and accomplish more than we used to accomplish in three-and-a-half," remarks one woman. "We do a lot on the fly—by phone, by e-mail. We actually spend more time in prayer and strategic thinking than we do in administration." This is normal for vital churches. "I mean, really," the same woman continued, "how much would actually stop in the church if we didn't have meetings? Not much. We only meet when there is no other, better way to get things done."

Pastors in vital churches do the best job of caring for themselves. With adequate rest and exercise, time for personal learning and reflection, and a disciplined spiritual life, these pastors model a balanced, well-integrated life for the congregation. Burnout, while not unheard of for pastors of vital churches, occurs much less frequently. Also, these pastors report the strongest sense of satisfaction, and believe their ministry aligns well with the sense of call that brought them to ministry in the first place. It is difficult to pinpoint cause and effect (do healthy pastors result in vital churches? or do vital churches result in healthy pastors?), but the correlation is strong: Vitality is shared by pastor and congregation alike.

Programmatic Design

There is no "fat" on the body of Christ in vital churches. Everything that is offered is offered for a clear reason: to help people become the body of Christ for the world. There are more programs in vital churches than in retrogressive congregations (less than in decaying and dystrophic churches), but they are strategically aligned with the mission, vision, and values of the congregation. Strategy is evident in vital churches, but unlike the other three types, strategic plans are living documents that help the congregation realize its goals and objectives.[4] Vital churches blend programs with services, projects, formation

4. My original research project was to examine planning processes in local congregations and annual conferences. Planning is widespread. Hundreds of United Methodist churches launch strategic planning processes each year, but only about one in ten actually follow the plan they develop. Some churches have engaged in four or five planning processes in the past decade. Planning ministry becomes the work instead of ministry itself. Vital congregations do the best job of planning, implementing the plan, evaluating the plan, and improving the plan.

groups, worship experiences, and leadership opportunities to create a holistic environment for faith development.

Program options tend to be limited in vital congregations. If a program is deemed valuable to faith formation and building the body of Christ, it is important that everyone has an opportunity to participate. There is a core curriculum in most vital congregations—a set of classes, groups, or experiences—that is central to the communal identity. There are essential components that shape the identity of the congregation. Everyone is expected to take part in them. They usually include Bible study, worship, witness, service, theology, leadership training, group process and dynamics, communication, and accountability. There are no assumptions that people already know how to do any of these things, but everyone is assisted in finding the best way to engage around these topics. Various programs are developed and redeveloped to promote shared knowledge and understanding. Programs are tools by which vital churches strengthen unity and stay focused.

Organizational Structure

Vital congregations have highly adaptive, deeply flexible structures that are continuously modified for peak efficiency. Form follows function, and function follows need. Vital churches know themselves very well; they know the gifts, resources, passions, skills, and knowledge with which they have to work, and through prayerful, thoughtful reflection, they have a clear sense of vision for their life and ministry together. With those two pieces in mind, leaders of vital congregations design and implement structures and processes that will most effectively use what is available to accomplish congregational goals and objectives. The visioning/futuring leaders dedicate most of their time to making sure the congregation is able to do the most with what they have. Because needs change, people grow and mature, knowledge expands, new gifts emerge, and God reveals new opportunities, no one structure is appropriate for all situations over time. The organization needs to be simple, lean, and flexible.

The structure of most vital churches closely resembles that of the retrogressive church—a small coordinating body with close ties to a few key functional areas. Work teams, committees, and councils work interdependently, but rarely end up in the same room at the same time. Information for decision and discussion is shared openly and freely, and often assignments are made on the fly. Because communication is so strong, everyone who is interested is kept "in the loop." Participation at all levels helps everyone feel involved, reducing the chance that someone may be left out. When people are productive and feel good about what is happening, they don't worry that they aren't represented on a committee or council. Very few people complain that they aren't in more meetings.

There are fewer complaints of feeling overburdened or burned out. Flexible structures allow people to work where they are comfortable and valued, and avoid less profitable work. Very few vital churches elect people to leadership terms. Instead, people are assigned to set functions, projects, or ministry areas where they share leadership. In only rare situations have these congregations met with resistance from their district superintendent. "We found that the key to modifying our structure was to work with our D.S. and not surprise him at Charge Conference," said one Church Council chair. When we laid out our proposed new structure, we gave a good rationale for every change we wanted to make, and made sure we didn't offend *The [Book of] Discipline* in any significant way. He [the D.S.] has been nothing but supportive . . . once we talked him into it."

There is no single, "right" model for church structure, but the common element in vital churches is "keep it simple." Expend only the necessary amount of time, energy, and resources to do the job right, and do away with everything else.

Leaders in vital congregations make friends with *The Book of Discipline*. Of the four church types, leaders in vital congregations know *The Discipline* most completely, use *The Discipline* most effectively, and gain the greatest benefit from the wealth of information it contains. Vital church leaders are best versed in the "Doctrinal Standards" and "Our Theological Task," "The Ministry of All Christians," and the "Social Principles" sections of *The Book of Discipline*. They also tend to be more conversant in Wesleyan theology and teaching, church history, and Christian writings throughout time. This is not an accident. Leaders in vital congregations are recruited and trained with an eye to spiritual maturity. Many vital churches provide the equivalent of a basic seminary education for their leadership, balancing the academic with the spiritual and the practical.

Money

It comes as no surprise that vital churches never want for money. Where people so deeply invest their hearts, their money follows (sounds biblical, doesn't it?). Vital congregations base their communal life in generosity, sacrifice, and service. Only a few vital churches gather any kind of pledge or financial commitment. Giving is so central to the messages of discipleship and steward-ship that there is no need.

Vital churches (like their retrogressive counterparts) do not use money-raising campaigns. These programs are aimed way below the commitment level of participants in vital churches. A number of leaders commented that they would be embarrassed to use a "stewardship" campaign for fear of offend-ing congregational members—not by asking too much, but by asking too little.

It is essential to the unity and common good of the congregation that every member gives sacrificially, which leads vital churches to take a unique approach to "deep pocket" givers. In most churches, there are one or two individuals or families of such means that they can make sizeable donations. In decaying and dystrophic (and a few retrogressive) churches, these gifts may account for a sig-nificant portion of the congregation's income. In vital churches, donors of large amounts are asked to establish specific funds, endowments, or trusts to fund specialized needs. By doing this, no individual's gift eclipses any other. Ministry is funded completely by the generosity and fine stewardship of the whole com-munity of faith, and exceptional gifts enable the congregation to expand the sphere of influence and do even more good in more places.

Vital congregations often manage huge amounts of money, all placed in active service to the ministry of the church. While unstable congregations often amass large reserves of capital, stable churches do not. The good that money can do in the short-term is too valuable to delay, Anyway, there's always more money out there.

Leaders in vital churches are very good at finding the money needed to fund God's work. They, too, have learned the lesson so many retrogressive lead-ers have learned: If you want money, you need to ask for it. Sitting in a small southwestern church, I listened in on a conversation about the congregation's scholarship fund. This church of no more than one hundred members pays a full four-year scholarship for a dozen underprivileged students! They send stu-dents to the college of their choice, regardless of the tuition. If the tuition is high, they solicit new donations. This church has quietly and anonymously been doing this for twenty years—paying for college for over sixty young men and women. The finance chair leaned across the table, shrugged, and said, "Hey, money's no big deal." This church's humble stewardship has improved the lives of dozens of individuals, their families, and their communities.

People talk about money in vital churches—not just the money they give, but their entire relationship with money. People talk about money problems, they pray about purchases and investments, and they counsel one another. Money talk is a normal part of the conversation, and is no more a cause for embarrassment or defensiveness than discussing the weather. Where people trust one another, this kind of candid exchange takes place. It is not unusual for congregations to help individual members financially in times of exceptional need. The openness to deal with the hard realities of money in the faith community hearkens back to the early church described in the book of Acts. While money is valued in vital churches for what it can do, money itself just isn't that important.

The Role of Worship in the Life of the Congregation

Worship is every bit as crucial to the life of the vital church as prayer, but not what is generally considered worship in other settings. While it is quite likely that you will find a fairly traditional one-hour Sunday morning service available in most vital churches, it is only one of many options. Vital congregations are three-dimensional. People are at different places in their journey of faith, they approach and experience God in different ways, and they have different needs and expectations. Leaders of vital churches long ago abandoned the naïve notion that one service would adequately allow a diverse and complex community to worship God.

And worshiping God is the point. In vital churches, worship is about God. It isn't a ploy to attract new members, or thinly disguised evangelism. It's not a teaching platform or a self-help center. It isn't entertainment, "edutainment," or a concert venue for frustrated musicians. It isn't a choir concert, a drama workshop, or a dancehall. Worship has an integrity all its own; it is the place where God's people come to honor, thank, and glorify God. It is a highly interactive experience. It is rarely performed for the congregation, but is performed with the congregation as an offering to God. There may be variations, but the focus is always on God, and on our relationship to God.

Vital congregations work to create an environment where everyone can encounter the risen Christ and experience the presence of God. Some people have a very intellectual faith, while others connect with God emotionally or viscerally. Some people express their faith through song, while others require silence. Some need time before the altar, some sitting quietly in the pew. Some have questions they need to raise; others want to hear a comforting word. Some wish to delve into Scripture with plenty of space and time to digest the richness of the word, while others desire to have the word of God illuminated and explained. These, and many other, expectations are all valid, and vital congregations find ways to honor them all. It is not unusual to find churches offering a dozen or more different worship experiences each week, in addition to the worship experiences in ongoing groups. In a variety of vital churches I heard the same statement, "Whenever we're together, we worship."

Communion is served most frequently in vital churches. The sacrament of the Lord's Supper is not a once a month add-on, as it seems to be in so many churches. Following the Wesleyan model, communion is served every week in many vital congregations. It is one more part of what gives the church its unique identity and creates oneness within the body of Christ.

Vital churches tend to be highly liturgical. Interactive rituals, practices, and traditions shape and define different worshiping groups within the fellowship. This is more than just a matter of taste; it is a matter of true spiritual diversity. One of the reasons that vital churches grow is that their variety of worship experiences appeals to a much broader audience of Christian believers, disciples, and leaders.

Talking with visitors to vital churches is an education in itself. Visitors are aware of a difference in the worship experience, even when they struggle to put it into words. A random sampling of responses from first time visitors to a number of vital churches offers these comments:

"That was what you expect church to be, but it so often isn't."

"There was a feeling . . . a feeling like you really are in the presence of God."

"There wasn't much to it. I mean, it wasn't crammed full of 'stuff' to do. But it actually felt like more happened, even though it wasn't so busy."

"I feel clean. It's like right after a good, long shower."

"I feel like the world is a better place. I just spent almost two hours marveling at how awesome God is."

"I could have stayed there for hours. That was wonderful."

"I am really impressed. I came with my mother, and didn't come that willingly. I don't have much use for church, but this was impressive. I would come back for this."

"I don't remember the last time I felt so close to God."

People have good experiences in churches from all four types, but consistently people share deep, meaningful responses from the experiences they have worshiping in vital churches.

The Role of Education in the Life of the Congregation

"If you aren't learning, you aren't Christian," proclaimed an octogenarian from a south- central vital church. Not every leader of a vital church might use these words, but they certainly model the sentiment. Vital churches are, in every sense of the word, learning organizations. The vision for Christian education begins at the cradle and extends to the grave. Many vital congregations have developed comprehensive lifelong learning plans. Leaders in these congregations work with individual members to draft personal learning plans, complete with milestones and goals along the way to measure progress. Groups in vital congregations read and discuss seminary level texts, study commentaries and books on theology, and explore great Christian writing. It was not unusual to find groups in vital congregations where homework is regularly assigned, and people write papers and take quizzes and tests. Some participants claimed they didn't work as hard in college or high school as they do in their church.

The guiding principle in vital churches is that in our life of faith, there is always more to learn, and that in our pursuit to become the body of Christ for the world, there is always room for improvement. This results in an incredibly high commitment to learning and spiritual formation. It is not optional; participants in vital congregations will pursue lifelong learning.

Almost all vital congregations spend time reflecting on the questions, "What does one need to know to grow in faith? To advance in discipleship? To be an effective steward? To be a Christlike leader?" As they clarify the essential knowledge in answer to each of these questions, they establish standards and criteria that form a core curriculum. They then design classes, small groups, and Bible studies that teach this core curriculum to the entire community of faith.

The learning plans for vital churches are well thought out, thoroughly planned, and impressively comprehensive. Participants in these churches develop a shared understanding, a common language, and a unified theological worldview that builds community and strengthens the body of Christ.

The Congregation's Relationship to the Community

Participants come to vital congregations to be transformed into the church (the body of Christ) for the community and world. Everything a vital church does reinforces a person's gifts, passions, and sense of Christian vocation to equip them to live his or her faith in the world. The ultimate goal is that every member of the congregation be the love and grace and voice of Christ to everyone they meet. This commitment makes a huge impact on the community surrounding a vital congregation.

Vital congregations continuously look for ways they may serve, support, and assist in the community. They reach out in Christian love, striving to make a positive impact wherever they can. This is not just in programs or in specific ministries, but in homes, workplaces, schools, shops, and on the street.

Participants in vital churches develop an awareness of need, a kind of radar that helps them focus on ways to live their faith in service to others. Every individual act of Christian service is celebrated as a facet of the ministry of the whole church. Vital congregations don't look to change the whole world, but they extend themselves to others that God might transform the world one act, one grace, and one person at a time.

Vital congregations are partnered with a wide variety of churches, agencies, and service organizations in their communities. They maximize their impact and influence by marrying their resources with the resources of other groups. If there is a good work being accomplished in a community, members of a vital church are generally involved.

And the circle of community is cast wide. Vital churches across the country have responded—not only with money, but with onsite work teams and advocates—to needs in Indonesia, Pakistan, Chile, and Louisiana. Vital churches are involved politically and socially, as well as spiritually. While not aligning with any party or platform, members of vital churches stand up for what they believe and they are encouraged to get involved in things they care about. One of the great successes of vital congregations is that they bridge articulated values (what we say is important) with lived values (the things we actually do). Communities benefit greatly from the ministries of vital churches.

The Congregation's Relationship to the Connectional System

Vital congregations support the connectional system, pay apportionments in full and on time, and provide leadership at the conference and district levels. They are knowledgeable about the doctrine and polity of The United

Methodist Church, *The Book of Discipline*, and Wesleyan theology. In many ways, they are the closest thing we have to the earliest Methodist congregations—highly motivated disciples, forming faith in accountability groups, who take their faith out into the highways and byways. Because they are so purely and traditionally Methodist, they are unique within the United Methodist system. Vital churches present many of the same challenges to the connection as retrogressive churches. Any congregation that establishes high expectations for their members requires a certain type of pastoral leader. Most pastors have not been adequately trained to lead a vital church. Dystrophic congregations have become the cultural norm, the benchmark by which "successful" churches are measured. Churches that do not judge themselves by numbers make little sense in our current reality.

The upside to our current dysfunction is that because vital churches are growing numerically, their pastors experience longer tenures. There is little motivation to move a pastor from a "successful" situation, and very few pastors in vital churches ever ask to be moved. Pastors of vital churches find it very difficult to go back to churches that have low expectations and a limited vision for ministry.

Vital churches, conversely, have a low tolerance for newly appointed pastors who won't get with the program and fit into a fully functioning faith community. Rarely does a pastor fight against a healthy church, but those situations do occur.[5] Usually, pastors are delighted to find themselves in vital churches, and experience revitalized hope, energy, and sense of purpose.

Vital churches proudly call themselves United Methodist and emphasize those aspects of our theology, polity, and doctrine worthy of the name. These congregations would be vital, regardless of denominational affiliation, but the fact is they are United Methodist and they let people know it.

Summarizing the Vital Reality

Vital churches are exciting, energizing, and enriching places. No one vital congregation in this study was doing everything perfectly, but they were making every effort to create God-focused, spiritually centered environments where

---

5. Leaders of one vital church contemplated paying their pastor to stay home Sundays, but they were able to work toward a new appointment instead, and little damage occurred in the one year he was with them.

every person, regardless of his or her location on the journey of faith, could flourish, thrive, and grow.

Vital churches are about God first, community second, and the individual last. Faith is a verb, not a noun. Vital churches enable people to balance the inward spiritual focus with a missional, evangelical outward practice. Complacency, laziness, and procrastination have no place in the vital church, nor does representative ministry. Never do you find ministry done by the few in the name of the many. Everyone in a vital church lives their ministry every day.

Accountability is paramount in the vital church. Making sure that what we say and what we do align perfectly is a high priority of the vital congregation. Vital churches are grounded in values, deep passions, and the relentless pursuit of God's will and vision for the faith community. Integrity is the best word to describe the vital church.

Many people find the description of the vital church compelling, but unrealistic. "It sounds great," one pastor told me, "but it would take a hundred years of non-stop work to get there. I can just hear what some people will say if we say we're going to hold them accountable or expect them to start doing certain things." Leaders in pursuit of vitality are not seeking it because it is easy, but because it is good and right.

"It is hard work—the hardest you will ever do—but where did we get the idea that church was supposed to be easy? We are talking about the meaning of life, eternal life, and a relationship with God, for crying out loud," a lay leader explained. "This should be easy?"

"People will put into it what they think it's worth," offered a small group leader and spiritual mentor. "I think there are a lot of people who starving for a whole different kind of life, a life with meaning, a *faith* with meaning. Sure, lots of people don't want what we have here, but you know what? A lot do. We are a church for those who are really, really serious about their faith. Too many people approach their faith as amateurs; we're the professionals."

Church isn't something a person can plug into an already full and otherwise demanding life. For participants in vital churches, church and life cannot be separated, and faith is never compartmentalized. The people are the church—every minute of every day. The body of Christ is incarnate, fulfilling the will of God as a faithful steward of all of God's creation.

CHAPTER 5

Pathways to Vitality

There is no potion, pill, or program that will give a congregation vitality. In our current, "we did it, you can do it too" church culture, it is sometimes hard to hear that there isn't some simple twelve-step approach to vitality. The reality is that it has taken us a long time to get where we are, and it will take time to get somewhere else. Whereas leaders in dystrophic churches often loudly proclaim, "Come see what we are doing. We will teach you how to be as effective as we are," leaders of vital churches stay strangely quiet. The power of their process to vitality is rooted in their own journey to self-discovery. "Every individual has a story," reflects one vital pastor. "Likewise, each church has its own story. People often look outside themselves for answers to all their problems, but ultimately they have to take responsibility for themselves. We looked outside for answers for years—and we found plenty—but they weren't the answers to *our* questions. We had to find those ourselves."

Another pastor framed it this way, "Work out your own salvation with fear and trembling. [Phil 2:12*b*] We have been to all the biggies [church training programs], spent thousands of dollars traveling to all these 'teaching' churches. We came home and one of the women on our team said, 'You know, this is all great stuff, but it has nothing to do with us.' From that moment forward, we stopped trying to be some other church and we learned to be the church God wants us to be."

One last comment further illustrates how different vital churches are from the other three types. "We don't have time to waste talking about how we got where we are. Time spent trying to teach others our process is time taken away from our ministry. The only way other churches can do what we did is figure out who they are, where God wants them, and how best to get there. That's our story—at least, the part of it that would be helpful to someone else. Anything more wastes our time and theirs."

There is no model of a vital church to emulate, no formula to follow, no prescription that will make all the problems go away. Following the body imagery adopted by so many vital congregations, vitality depends on good diet, regular exercise, adequate rest and renewal, and meaningful engagement. The variety of healthy food, rigorous exercise, restful pursuits, and meaningful activity is almost endless. The specific combination will vary greatly from church body to church body, but discipline and commitment to these four areas will move the body toward true health and vitality.

When thinking about becoming more vital, it is important to understand where you are starting from. The Vitality Assessment contained in appendix 1 was developed by the congregations in this study to help churches begin to understand where they are, and the steps they can take to move toward vitality. In the broadest terms, the following conceptual frame helps congregational leaders think about where to turn their attention first.

+	RETROGRESSIVE	VITAL
Depth of Focus	DECAYING	DYSTROPHIC
–	—	**Breadth of Focus** +

Vital congregations balance the breadth of their focus (the ministries they offer and the people they serve) with an impressive depth of focus (the level of immersion and saturation in the ministries). This balance creates an incredibly rich, transformative experience for participants.

Dystrophic congregations offer enormous breadth, but with little depth. Participants may sample a diverse selection of experiences, moving from program to program, getting only as involved as they choose.

Retrogressive congregations offer narrow breadth, but what they do offer is very deep. Participants find themselves immersed in all-consuming, all-encompassing ministry.

Decaying congregations offer little breadth, with very little depth. Participants attend programs with few demands and low expectations.

There are exceptions in every category, but in general terms, unstable congregations should explore ways to increase the depth of focus in one or two key areas. A focus on depth, creating rich, textured, multi-layered formation experiences, is a strong stabilizing factor, and moves a congregation toward vitality. Where a congregation has a deep focus in one or two areas, leaders should explore options to expand the ministry in one or two more key areas for spiritual formation, and apply the same level of focus as it widens its offerings.

This chapter focuses on the broad areas in which a congregation can start to work. Where a church begins is not as important as the congregational leaders' commitment to work diligently and honestly in whatever area they choose. It is important to keep in mind that the four church types described in the preceding chapters are composites, or pure types, cultivated from the many shared stories. I encountered no congregations that were vital in every respect, nor did I find any congregations in total decay. Every retrogressive church had small growing areas, and almost every dystrophic church had pockets of vitality, retrogression, and decay. The following seven focus areas are identified by vital churches as those critical areas that emerged as the greatest challenges to vitality.[1] Unless and until the church dealt with these issues, health and vitality was impossible. The critical focus areas for congregations seeking vitality are: thinking holistically about the congregation, balancing inward and outward focus, pursuing lifelong learning, developing ways to measure and evaluate impact,

---

1. Forty-one of the vital churches in the project prioritized a list of fifteen factors. Seven factors were identified as critically important by 75% or more of the respondents. None of the other eight factors was identified by more than 36% as critical.

establishing standards with accountability, becoming developmentally complex, and creating transparency.

Thinking Holistically about the Congregation

In a consumeristic, highly individualistic society, putting community first is a radical counter-cultural message. Most people come to church so that they might be served and receive benefit. This is one small aspect of church (being served) but it is not why the church exists. Putting the needs and will of the whole congregation ahead of those of individuals lays the foundation upon which a vital church may be built. No one person is allowed undue influence. No one voice predominates, and no one position holds the deciding vote. The metaphor of the body of Christ is more than a nice idea; it is the guiding principle around which the congregation develops a covenant for life together. Paul's guidance in 1 Corinthians 12 reminds us that there is a place in the body for everyone, no part is more valuable than any other, no part can decide to do without the others, and that Christ is the head of the body. Members of vital churches ask, "What is best for us," instead of "What is best for me?"

Fellowship takes on a whole new depth of meaning in vital churches. Fellowship is opportunity to create true community, one in heart, mind, and spirit. Fellowship is more than passing time together. It is a process of becoming one. As congregations unify and coalesce, rich and fertile explorations of values, worldviews, passions, hopes, and dreams emerge. Opportunity to discuss these fundamental issues in a safe, encouraging Christian environment weaves individuals into true community. As the community comes first in the hearts and minds of the participants, a new level of being church surfaces.

Dystrophic congregations can begin to explore ways they perpetuate an individualistic approach to faith and begin to challenge it and invite passive members to think and grow communally. This is true for decaying churches as well, though many declining and unstable churches are already a tight-knit group. Still, there is a great challenge in putting the needs of the community before individual needs. Many decaying congregations suffer because only one or two people feel that their needs, their desires, and their opinions should count. Retrogressive congregations need to become a little more permeable—allowing space for newcomers to enter the congregation. It is too easy for retrogressive congregations to make the definition of community too narrow and exclusive.

Balancing Inward and Outward Focus

The vast majority of contemporary United Methodist Churches are inwardly focused. The church building is the center of the Christian universe. We commit massive resources to get more and more people to come to us. From these church centers we might dispatch an occasional work team or missionary (or a check to support same), but in most people's minds, church is the place to which we go.

Vital congregations view the place to which they go as that place where they are trained and equipped to be the church in the world. There is a healthy, balanced approach to being the church: coming together to learn, going forth to serve. They practice acts of Piety (praying, worshiping, studying, sharing) as well as acts of Mercy (serving, healing, caring, and visiting). Leaders of vital congregations make little distinction between the two.

One simple way to begin thinking about balancing the inward and outward focus is to be very clear about who benefits from what your congregation does. If your congregation offers Bible study, how does this Bible study benefit people outside the fellowship? How do people behave differently in the world after they attend worship? How does the congregation benefit when a youth team goes on a mission trip? How do families and friends benefit from the participants of a *Companions in Christ* group? In other words, what is the outward and visible sign of the inward and spiritual graces of your congregation?

It is easiest for decaying and dystrophic congregations to look at something big and basic, like worship or Sunday school. If the church is a placid pool, and worship is the stone tossed in, what are the ripples that result? Beyond just the person in the pew, what difference does worship make in the lives of others? How are people empowered and improved by the experience? (How do you know?) With retrogressive congregations, it is well to ask how activities are growing faith and developing spiritual maturity. Often, participants in retrogressive churches find they are too busy to pray, read the Bible, or attend to their own needs.

Pursuing Lifelong Learning

Most adults in our churches see education and learning as optional. A small percentage of the congregation attends Sunday school, Bible study, or topical discussion groups. Very few pursue technical skill development. Many left focused, intentional learning behind when they left high school or college. This is not true of vital churches.

Promoting a love of learning and developmental plans are high priorities in vital congregations. Vital churches have a clear picture of what it means to be a Christian believer, a Christian disciple, a Christian leader, and the body of Christ. They work hard to develop a broad-based understanding of what people need to know to progressively grow in their Christian faith. There is a lot to learn if we want to become like Jesus the Christ. In many vital churches, more people attend Christian learning experiences than formal worship services each week.

Learning is both an individual and shared experience. Groups work through complex and challenging material to deepen their faith.[2] Vital churches tend not to read about the modern church or the latest Christian "best sellers," but source material. Studies in prayer, church history, theology, mysticism, spiritual discipline, and social reform are most common. Groups read Wesley's sermons and writings, Barth and Bonhoeffer, Spong and Borg, Augustine and Aquinas. They don't shy away from the "heavy hitters." It is impressive to see entire congregations tackle books that many pastors avoid.

The advice to all churches—decaying, dystrophic, and retrogressive—is find a short, simple piece, such as Steve Manskar's excellent treatment of John Wesley's "A Plain Account of Christian Perfection" in *A Perfect Love*[3], and have everyone read it, discuss it, and ask, "What else do we need/want to know?" Begin where there is energy and hunger. Start with those most willing, encourage those who are reluctant, and don't worry too much about those not interested. Either they will come around as the movement gains momentum, or they won't.

Developing Ways to Measure and Evaluate Impact

"Small minds count, grand minds measure," reads an anonymous quote carved in a stone near Athens, Greece. Leaders in vital churches could not agree more.

---

2. One United Methodist Women's Ruth Circle (seventy-five and older) in a small rural Midwestern town studied together Ched Myer's *Binding the Strong Man*, a seminary level political commentary on the Gospel of Mark. A blue collar men's group in the plains states tackled the writings of Meister Eckhart. These examples are not unusual in vital churches.

3. Discipleship Resources, 2001.

It is not that quantitative measures are not important in the right places, but what vital churches measure is growth as the body of Christ. Just as weight is one measure of health in the human body, size is one measure of health in the church (though this metaphor breaks down quickly since we have so many churches trying to gain weight). But, it probably isn't one of the most important measures. Vital churches develop qualitative metrics that measure:

number of lives touched in a positive way

number of people served

evolution of participants' understanding of Scripture and theology

healthy lifestyle changes of the participants

improvements in relationships

levels of connection and commitment to the faith community

These are just a sample of the kinds of things that vital churches learn to measure. These standards take them away from a "growth as more" mentality, to a "growth as depth" mentality.

Leaders in vital churches use these measurements as they envision ways to improve and become more effective in the future. By understanding how lives are changing and the ways God is transforming the world through the congregation, vital congregational leaders chart the next steps that further build up the body of Christ.

Presented in this straightforward way, it sounds like no great challenge to shift from quantitative to qualitative measurement, but nothing could be further from the truth. Quantitative measurement is easy; qualitative measurement is hard. Leaders in every vital church confess that they struggle with qualitative measures, but that while they are difficult, they are necessary. Vitality depends on them.

Every church should identify one thing worth measuring in a qualitative way. Figure out what to measure, why it is important, what it will tell you, and how you will determine whether it is improving or not. Then, and only then, figure out how you will measure it and what you will do with that you learn. Start small, learn from the effort, and then move on to include more and more things.

Establishing Standards with Accountability

There will be nothing more difficult than getting serious about discipleship and establishing standards to which members will be held accountable. Many people feel that the church has no right to expect anything from them. Decades of focus by denominational leaders on congregational, rather than connectional, growth has resulted in a church where the person who joins defines their own participation. It is evident that many people attending church do so as a matter of convenience, while a significant number believe that it is enough merely to have their name recorded on a church's membership roll. Some of the fastest growing megachurches are designed around low-level demands and low expectations. Mainline churches are guilty of continuously relaxing standards so that less motivated individuals will not become disillusioned and leave the church.

When a congregation makes membership *mean* something, it opens the door to all kinds of unpleasantness. Leaders of vital churches liken it to a storm that rages through the congregation, washes away the deadwood, does some significant damage to long standing relationships, and plunges the congregation into a period of grieving. Sounds like fun, doesn't it? There are some pastors and laity who believe that it is unthinkable to let people leave the church, let alone make them want to leave. But, just as many people who believed in Jesus chose not to follow him in the first century, so many who believe in Jesus today will balk when it comes to making the commitment to live as Christian disciples. "It comes to a point," reflected one Church Council chair, "where you have to ask, 'Will we serve the best in our congregation, or continue to pander to the worst? Will we do all in our power to please God, or will we do all in our power to please people?' We couldn't, in good conscience, look each other in the eye anymore. We knew we had to make some changes. It hurt a lot, but it was the right thing to do."

Vital churches define a set of "non-negotiables," things they believe describe the least a person must do to be considered a member of the church. Among the things they have identified are:

prayer with other members of the congregation every week

development of a personal devotional life (to which they are held accountable)

participation in some form of communal worship each week

participation in some form of spiritual formation group (Sunday school, Bible study, accountability group, or discussion group)

participation in some form of Christian service, outreach, or witness every week (to which they are held accountable)

Individual congregations may have other criteria, but these emerge as the basics in every setting. What happens when someone fails to keep covenant with the basics? They are removed from the active membership roles until they meet the base criteria.

Establishing standards says nothing about who can come to church, join a Sunday school class, be visited in the hospital, or attend a fellowship supper. Anyone can come to the church and receive the blessing and benefit of its ministry. But membership has both its privileges and its responsibilities. Voice and vote belong to those who give of themselves in a meaningful way to build up and strengthen the body of Christ. People earn their right to lead and have a say in the future of the congregation. Not one leader from any vital church regretted the hard and painful work of setting standards. Most report it to be the best decision the church ever made.

Retrogressive congregations are already very proficient at setting standards and holding members accountable. Leaders in decaying and dystrophic congregations generally don't think in these terms. One helpful first step is to establish a set of criteria for the core leadership of the congregation—a covenantal set of "basics" to which leaders hold one another accountable. As the leaders model the baseline for the congregation, they can credibly expand the circle to include the congregation. It is a very simple matter to justify membership criteria biblically, and so a series of Bible studies on what it means to be the body of Christ is advisable. Include the congregation in the development process. Have conversations about what are fair and legitimate expectations for people who want to be a part of a community of faith. This is not the kind of thing that works well if it is simply imposed from on high. Just as people need to work into more aggressive forms of exercise over time, congregations need to work into appropriate levels of accountable discipleship over time.

Becoming Developmentally Complex

At what point do people stop growing in their faith? By all appearances in most churches, it is somewhere around age thirteen, shortly following confirmation.

Adults are treated as though they are all in approximately the same place in their journey of faith. One or two forms of worship are offered, beginner level Sunday school classes meet weekly, and simple, non-challenging sermons are preached. The flaw in this scenario is blatantly obvious. Members of any congregation are at a wide variety of places in the faith journey, and a simple "one size fits all" approach cannot be effective. Simply adding more basic experiences serves the needs of the novice, but does little to actually deepen people's faith and serve them as they evolve spiritually.

Vital congregations intentionally target at least three distinct levels of Christian development—what one congregation designates "the Believer," "the Disciple," and "the Spiritual Leader" levels. "There is an infancy, an adolescence, and a maturity to every life of faith," says one lay leader. "They aren't clean categories, and you never completely leave one as you grow into the next, but there are definite differences. You dishonor everyone when you treat everyone the same."

"I guess you could say this is my fault," confessed one man sheepishly. "I listened to a sermon on the Prodigal Son, and it was like every other sermon I ever heard on the Prodigal Son, you know? I stood up in my Sunday school class and said something like, 'I cannot do this anymore! Doesn't this ever go anywhere? What is the point? There has got to be more than just these simple morality stories!' I thought people would boo me, criticize me, but instead, almost everyone started nodding their heads. It turns out, just about everyone I knew was fed up and tired of the same old thing. We asked the pastor to help us find things that were more challenging, and she did." There are a lot of people in our churches starving for something more challenging, and vital congregations find ways to feed the hunger.

Pastors often complain that they aren't able to teach to their congregations what they learned in seminary. This is a result of the long-standing practice of pandering to the lowest common denominator. Nominal Christians rarely want the comfort of a children's Sunday school theology challenged by critical thinking. The level of scholarship and theological reflection presented in seminary is terrifying to an unexamined faith. An immature faith is understandable in new Christians, but it is an abdication of responsibility to allow people to stay there. Vital congregations conceptualize a multilayered, developmental Christianity, and create an environment where everyone, no matter where they are in their faith journey, can find spiritual nurture, nourishment, and promotion to higher levels.

Decaying congregations can begin to create a developmental model by differentiating the needs between the most deeply committed members of the congregation, and those of the less committed. It is a simple process to make sure that adequate experiences exist that help people at both levels evolved spiritually. Priority should be given to the spiritually mature (since the majority of decaying church programs already focus on the beginner level).

Many dystrophic congregations believe they already have a developmental model, when in fact they do not. It is important to look not only at what is offered, but also at what results from what is offered. Beginners tend to soak up information and experiences, but may not do much with it. Disciples are integrating faith with action, beginning to live their faith in meaningful ways. Leaders are committed to service and sacrifice. How behaviors and attitudes change are the best indicators of how well a congregation meets the developmental needs of individuals.

Retrogressive churches may benefit most by reevaluating the beginner level. Often retrogressive churches hold participants to a high level of learning, and offer little for the spiritual novice. Many newcomers to the faith, attracted by the missional focus of a congregation, find no place where they fit in. Vital congregations make space for everyone at the table—offering a wide variety of dishes to feed the widest variety of spiritual hungers.

Creating Transparency

No matter what category a church finds itself in, communication is named as one of the most important issues facing the congregation. Vital churches are masters of good communication. In vital churches, anyone can know anything about the church. When a congregation is a unified body, the whole congregation deals with the most important issues—even cases of financial misappropriation or clergy sexual misconduct. In a truly loving, caring, Christian environment, nothing needs be hidden or obfuscated.

If there are things happening in a congregation that leaders feel should be kept secret, it is a reflection on the trust and honesty level of the church environment. Vital congregations do not wait for trust before they share information; they develop a policy of full disclosure as a way to build trust. They also create a wide variety of ways, places, and times where information may be shared and discussed.

Vital churches prefer dialogue over monologue. They do not depend on newsletters, letters, bulletins, and e-mails to share information. They create opportunities where conversation can occur. In dialogue, people come to a meeting of minds in ways they may not through one-way communication.

"I came from a church where we had a 'what's said here, stays here' policy in all the committees. Decisions were clouded in all kinds of intrigue. Leaders sweated in fear that certain people in the church would find out what we were talking about. It was sick. Here, there is no secrecy. In fact, we're encouraged to talk about what we do and talk about in our teams. The only people who don't know what's going on are the people who choose not to know, and even they know more than they want to." Full disclosure, transparency, open communication—these are cornerstones of the vital church.

Unstable congregations guard information and have dysfunctional communication networks. Often, delicate information gets spread far and wide (usually erroneously) while public knowledge languishes in the minds of too few. Gossip runs rampant, leading to misinformation, unnecessary conflict, and institutional ignorance. There is only one way to improve communication, and that's to improve communication. Be clear about what needs to be known, who needs to know it (in the case of healthy churches, everyone), and multiple methods for dialogue. Make a conscious decision to be open about everything and forbid secretive or disingenuous behavior. If there is controversial or delicate information to share, work intentionally and diligently to find the best way to share it.

Conclusion

"Re-vital-izing" the church requires support at all levels. This book focuses primarily on that which happens within the individual congregation, but in The United Methodist Church we are a part of a connectional system, with annual conference responsibilities, and district supervision. We have an itinerant appointment system that reallocates pastoral leadership throughout the system. Developing vital congregations requires the commitment of our conference leaders to work in partnership with congregations making this crucial journey. One of the strongest mitigating factors for growth is the length of the pastoral appointment. No church reached vitality with a pastoral appointment of less than seven years. The success of a vital congregation does not rest on the pastor's shoulders, but pastoral changes are incredibly disruptive to the overall momentum of a congregation. The journey toward vitality takes time, and having a positive, productive partnered relationship between congregation and pastoral leader is a great asset. Many decaying churches are locked into a downward spiral because they have pastors for only a year or two at a time. If a congregation has the potential to break free from its negative inertia, it must have a pastor who will stay for the long, hard process to come. The healthiest churches in this research sample were those with pastors in place for seven to ten years.

The decision to leave pastors in place for seven to ten years, and not leave pastors in place much longer than this, poses significant challenges to our present appointment processes. It depends upon a vision for vitality that is contrary to our current desire for active, large, impressive church centers. Denominational leaders may need to reevaluate itinerancy in light of the critical demands of ministry in the twenty-first century.

Every bishop and cabinet I meet holds a deep commitment and desire to make good appointments. None of our leaders take the appointment process lightly. Every effort is made to make good matches between pastoral gifts and congregational need. There are cases where the match is clearly not going to work, and changes must be made. This is self-evident, and it is much more art than science. Annual Conference leadership needs to be as clear about the mission, vision, purpose, and values of a local congregation as the congregation is itself. Helping the local church become vital is what most annual conferences are all about.

Every United Methodist church can work to increase stability and strengthen sustainability. It may require slow, incremental, "baby steps," but it can be done. The story of every vital church describes a path from dystrophy or decay through retrogression. The elimination of non-essential effort, the prioritization of work that forms faith, establishing standards of participation, and the flattening of the organizational structure almost guarantee a short-term loss of less active, less engaged members. This is not a message that will attract a lot of support. We may say "less is more," but we don't seem to mean it when it comes to the church. It isn't clear when having 1,000 passive Christians (300 of them inactive) became preferable to a dozen highly motivated disciples, but that shift definitely occurred in North American mainline United Methodism.

At the heart of the issue is a very important question: Who do we think we are? If the church is essentially about us, then it doesn't much matter what our driving motivations and values are. We can do pretty much anything we want to: build huge buildings with art and statuary, the latest digital technology, and stadium-worthy parking lots. We can go on TV and radio and rent billboards. We can launch leadership academies and create a cult of church celebrities. All of this is fine if the church is about us; except we're United Methodists. And even before that, we're Christians. The church is not now, nor has it ever been, about us.

Certainly, the church is *for* us, and at its very best it *is* us, but it isn't *about* us. It's about God and God's vision for all creation. If any church is truly vital, its vitality comes from God, and it is the unrelenting focus on God that keeps it vital.

APPENDIX 1

Congregational Vitality Assessment Survey

In each category, select the response that most closely describes your congregation:

Growth Factors

1. Membership in our congregation has:			
declined for the past 3 years	declined in the past year	increased in the past year	increased for the past 3 years

2. Attendance in worship has:			
declined for the past 3 years	declined in the past year	increased in the past year	increased for the past 3 years

3. Participation in Christian education opportunities have:			
declined for the past 3 years	declined in the past year	increased in the past year	increased for the past 3 years

4. The number of non-members served by our congregation has:			
declined for the past 3 years	declined in the past year	increased in the past year	increased for the past 3 years

5. The percentage of *active* members in our congregation is between:			
0-55%	56-70%	71-85%	86-100%

6. The number of *distinctly different* worship service options in our congregation is:			
1	2	3-5	more than 5

7. The number of ongoing outreach ministries of our congregation is:			
0-3	4-9	10-15	more than 15

8. Financial support through participant giving for the past three years has:			
declined	increased less than 10%	increased 10-25%	increased more than 25%

9. Awareness of our ministry and mission throughout the surrounding community is:			
very low	low	high	very high

10. Visitors to our congregation:			
generally come only once	usually return at least once	usually return regularly	generally become involved in the ongoing ministry

11. We contact visitors:			
not at all	by letter or phone within a week	personally, within 36 hours	personally, within 6 hours

12. We offer age-specific ministries to:			
1 or 2 age groups	3 age groups	4 age groups	more than 4 age groups

Totals for numbers 1 – 12:			
Column A =	Column B =	Column C =	Column D =
x –5	x –3	x +3	x +5
A. =	B. =	C. =	D. =
A. + B. =		C. + D. =	
Growth Plot Point (AB/CD combined) =			

Stability Factors

13. The percentage of active members in leadership positions is:			
0-15%	15-35%	35-55%	55-100%

14. The percentage of the congregation with a clear, shared understanding of the mission of the UMC is:			
less than 10%	10-40%	41-75%	more than 75%

15. The percentage of the congregation with a clear, shared vision for ministry is:			
less than 10%	10-40%	41-75%	more than 75%

16. Hours leadership spends per week in meetings (planning, governing, staff, etc.)			
more than 5	4-5	3-4	less than 3

17. Hours leadership spends per week together in Christian formation (prayer, study, faith sharing, etc.)			
less than 3	3-4	4-5	more than 5

18. Percentage of total ministry and program taking place offsite (away from church building):			
less than 10%	10-20%	20-30%	more than 30%

19. We address the financial needs of the congregation using:			
no special efforts	annual campaigns	regular asking/appeals	conversation/ relationships

20. Our primary measure of effectiveness or success is:			
growth in numbers attending	growth in numbers of those involved in leadership	growth in numbers of people served	growth in the spiritual commitment and faith formation in people's lives

21. Worship, education, fellowship, and service opportunities are:

independent program emphases of the congregation	loosely related in focus, but developed independently	coordinated to support the primary focus of our congregation	tightly integrated, designed and implemented collaboratively

22. The number of hours the pastor(s) works per week – on average:

80-70	70-60	60-50	50-40

23. The location of our church facility is:

vital to the success of our ministry	very important to the success of our ministry	nominally important to the success of our ministry	unrelated to the success of our ministry

24. The charisma, energy, and image of the pastor(s) is:

vital to the success of our ministry	very important to the success of our ministry	nominally important to the success of our ministry	unrelated to the success of our ministry

Totals for numbers 13 – 24:

Column A =	Column B =	Column C =	Column D =
x –5	x –3	x +3	x +5
A. =	B. =	C. =	D. =
A. + B. =		C. + D. =	
Stability Plot Point (AB/CD combined) =			

Instructions

1. Fill out the Assessment Survey, completing both Growth Factors and Stability Factors sections.

2. Total the number of marked boxes in each column under Growth Factors and enter the number in the boxes marked "A" "B" "C" and "D."

3. Multiply the number in each box by the appropriate factor (-5, -3, +3, +5).

4. Enter new total in the spaces provided.

5. Combine A + B and C + D.

6. Combine A/B + C/D to yield your Growth Plot Point.

7. Total the number of marked boxes in each column under Stability Factors and enter the number in the boxes marked "A" "B" "C" and "D."

8. Multiply the number in each box by the appropriate factor (-5, -3, +3, +5).

9. Enter new total in the spaces provided.

10. Combine A + B and C + D.

11. Combine A/B + C/D to yield your Stability Plot Point.

12. Using the chart below, find the approximate point along the horizontal (growth) line that corresponds to your Growth Plot Point.

13. Using the chart below, find the approximate point along the vertical (stability) line that corresponds to your Stability Plot Point.

14. By extending lines from the two points (Growth and Stability), determine where the two lines intersect and make a mark. This will locate your congregation in one of the four quadrants.

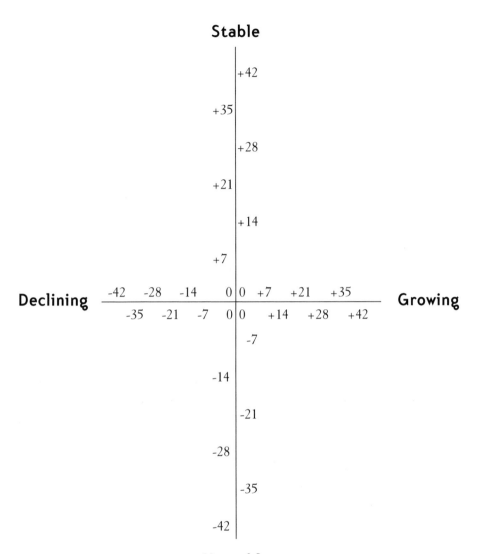

Using the Information

The four quadrants reflect different current realities for the congregation. Using labels drawn from the science of biology, there are four basic congregational "types":

Vital	Congregations that are both stable and growing
Dystrophic	Congregations that are growing, but unstable
Decaying	Congregations that are both declining and unstable
Retrogressive	Congregations that are declining, but stable

The primary thesis of this planning assessment is that all congregations desire to both grow and become stable. Vitality (not mere growth in numbers) is the desired reality of each congregation.

This assessment tool not only locates the congregation in a "current reality" but also offers helpful information to use to move toward vitality. Individual factors may invite a congregational leadership team to focus on internal ministries, external ministries, leadership practices, financial processes, attendance numbers, service numbers, hospitality issues, or pastoral practices and expectations. Here are some suggestions for ways to interpret this tool to create an improvement plan:

1. Don't think in "good/bad" terms. A qualitative value judgment is *not* intended. Gaining insights into current reality offers a starting point for improvement. Attempt to be the best church you can be wherever you find yourself.

2. The closer you are to a line (growth or stability zero ("0") point), the easier it is to move toward vitality. For that reason, build on your strengths.

3. Look to -3s before -5s. It is easier to convert a -3 to a +3 and thereby move toward vitality.

4. Work on one factor at a time. Keep energy and focus where it can do the most good.

5. For decaying congregations, it is much easier to build on stability factors than growth factors. Worry less about numbers (quantity) and more about sustainability (quality).

6. For retrogressive congregations, the path to greatest growth is to strengthen stability factors. The majority of retrogressive congregations that move to vitality do so because of the passion and integrity with which they pursue their mission. People are attracted to the mission and vision.

7. For dystrophic congregations, building on stability factors usually requires a radical reorientation of current structure, leadership styles and processes, and focus. In many cases, when dystrophic congregations get serious about building stability, there is a period of retrogression before moving to vitality. This is *normal*. (Don't sweat the numbers in the short term!)

8. For vital congregations, leadership reports that as numbers increase, it becomes harder to stay focused on stability factors (success is often more dangerous than failure!). Stability factors are critical to vitality. Make sure to keep stability factors *in balance* with growth factors.

APPENDIX 2

Resources Employed by the Four Church Types

The church/church leadership publishing industry is supported by decaying and dystrophic churches—which is no surprise, since they account for 83% of all United Methodist Churches (with approximately similar percentages in most mainline Protestant denominations[1]). Due to the popularity of the dystrophic model since the mid-1970s, the short, simple church growth writings of Lyle Schaller, Bill Easum, Ken Callahan, Michael Slaughter, Adam Hamilton, Bill Hybels, Rick Warren, and others have found a willing audience. These books offer a form of hope to church leaders unclear on what their call and purpose is all about. Unable to figure out how to "be church" on their own, these leaders look to outside sources to find out. Evidence that these resources don't work to build vitality comes from the fact that the market for them never seems to shrink.

Now, before it looks as though I am pointing fingers, let me be completely honest. Only dystrophic and decaying churches reported using the resources developed by Discipleship Resources. Unstable churches also named Dan Dick, Craig Miller, Herb Miller, Herb Mather, and Carol Krau as authors they read. The point is not to indict either the authors or their works, but to say that healthy, stable congregations do not rely on these types of resources—either to get healthy, or stay healthy.

Decaying and dystrophic congregations also rely heavily on programmatic resources—DISCIPLE, *Companions in Christ*,[2] Igniting Ministries, *40 Days of*

---

1. Based purely upon anecdotal responses received from mid- and top-level judicatory leaders. No research has been done on these four church types outside of The United Methodist Church.

2. DISCIPLE Bible studies (Cokesbury) and *Companions in Christ* (Upper Room) were the only two United Methodist-produced resources regularly named by all four types. Many vital and retrogressive congregations use and respect these two wonderful resources.

Purpose, Walk to Emmaus, *Christian Believer*, among them. Most of these resources are aimed at deepening the faith of less mature believers, so they have a limited appeal to more stable congregations.

Dystrophic and decaying churches also follow fads pretty faithfully. Eugene Peterson's *The Message*; Bruce Wilkinson's *Prayer of Jabez*; and Rick Warren's *The Purpose Driven Life*, found widespread use in unstable congregations, and virtually no use in stable congregations. Currently, the Emergent Church movement is "hot," and decaying and dystrophic churches are ravenously consuming the products of this growing cottage industry.

So, if vital and retrogressive churches don't read these books or use these resources, what do they use? The simplest answer is that they use primary sources, and primary among these is the Bible. Without meaning to be glib, many dystrophic and decaying churches have barely a passing relationship with Scripture. It may be read from the lectern in worship (often substituting a paraphrase like *The Message* for a solid translation) or a passage used in a Sunday school class, and occasionally a small group might immerse themselves in a thirty-four week study, but the Bible itself is not widely read or understood by a significant number of people in the church. This is not true in vital churches. (Retrogressive congregations are divided about evenly). Participants in vital congregations are far and away the most biblically literate United Methodists.

In addition to the Bible, vital congregations spend a lot of time studying Christian history, theology, the writings of the saints and mystics, as well as the contemporary writings of Marcus Borg, Elaine Pagels, Jim Wallis, Daniel Berrigan, Wendell Berry, Robert Wuthnow, and C. Michael Thompson. They are also well read in thinkers outside of the Christian tradition such as Bernie Glassman, Margaret Wheatley, Ken Wilber, Chogyam Trungpa, and Peter Senge. For the most part, vital and retrogressive churches do not use many prepackaged materials.

Vital churches study history and heritage more than other church types as well. They read John Wesley, George Whitfield, and the study the "Our Theological Task" and "Social Principles" sections of *The Book of Discipline*. They are familiar with the hymnody of Charles Wesley, as well as the rich musical tradition so central to the Methodist church.

There are some authors that transcend church type—finding audiences across the entire spectrum. C. S Lewis, Dietrich Bonhoeffer, Richard Foster, Parker Palmer, and Henri Nouwen are all well read and well respected throughout the denomination.

APPENDIX 3

Giving Patterns of the Four Church Types

One way to compare and contrast the four church types is through the giving patterns, which are distinctly different for each. The following analysis looks at both dollar-per-member giving as well as percentage giving. The methodology is to divide weekly giving to the church into four equal tiers calculated based on the range between the highest per week gift and the lowest per week gift in every church.

Example: If the highest gift per week is $200 and the lowest is $0, then subtract the lowest number from the highest and divide by four. In this example, the four tiers would be from bottom to top: $0-$50, $51-$100, $101-$150, and $151-$200.

The number in each box represents the percentage of the congregation falling within that tier based on the congregations sampled in this study.

Dollar-per-member	Decaying	Dystrophic	Retrogressive	Vital
1st Tier	6%	4%	58%	48%
2nd Tier	11%	16%	24%	23%
3rd Tier	15%	19%	12%	21%
4th Tier	68%	61%	6%	8%

In the case of percentage giving (instead of actual dollar-per-member), the four tiers are: 0–3.3%, 3.4%–6.6%, 6.7%–9.9%, 10%+

% Giving	Decaying	Dystrophic	Retrogressive	Vital
1st Tier (10%+)	5%	11%	71%	60%
2nd Tier (6.7–9.9%)	21%	19%	13%	28%
3rd Tier (3.4–6.6%)	35%	31%	5%	9%
4th Tier (0–3.3%)	38%	39%	11%	3%

The actual figures are less important than the trends they identify: The majority of givers in vital and retrogressive churches give from the top two tiers, while the majority of givers in decaying and dystrophic churches give from the lowest tier. A few "deep-pocket" givers in decaying and dystrophic congregations overcome the shortfall this causes (or not, in many cases), but this results in a low level of sustainability. These churches follow the Law of Pareto: 20% of the cause generates 80% of the effects, or in the case of the church, 20% of the participants provide 80% of the support.

This is not true of retrogressive and vital congregations. Giving is a deeply integrated component of the spiritual life. In retrogressive congregations, tithing is not set as a goal, but for a significant number of people, it is the base upon which they build. John Wesley, who set tithing as the "minimum" standard of giving for the people called Methodists, would be proud. The support of the ministries and mission of the community of faith is shared by a significant majority of the participating members. This explains why all but one of the churches in the retrogressive and vital quadrants do not rely on annual giving campaigns: they don't need to. Money is of secondary importance to growing as Christian disciples, stewards, and leaders. As people grow in their faith, they grow in their investment of time, energy, and material resources. Where the heart is, the treasure follows.

When wide bases of supporters fund a ministry, it never becomes dependent on the kindness, commitment, or whim of an individual giver. Many decaying, and a few dystrophic congregations, find themselves financial hostages to an individual or family. Any time the giver is displeased, he or she merely threatens to withhold financial support. This is one more insidious guise of a toxic influencer posing as a faithful church member.

The role money plays in each church type is different. For decaying congregations, money means survival, and as soon as there is a deficit, it becomes an all important and consuming emphasis. Dystrophic churches are ravenous beasts, requiring incredible amounts of money simply to support building, staff, upkeep, and overhead. Growth costs a lot of money, and a thriving church must aggressively solicit funds. Retrogressive churches are driven by their passion, and all resources are aligned to achieve the greatest good. When a church orients itself in mission to meet a cultural or global need, there is always more that can be done, and money is a powerful tool in the ongoing endeavor. Because giving is tied to passion and getting good results, people are highly motivated to give. In vital churches, money is one aspect of the total person growing in relationship to God and directed by God's will to be faithful stewards. Because giving is so deeply integrated into the vital church worldview, virtually no one associated with a vital church gives at less than a substantial and sacrificial level.

APPENDIX 4

Learning Issues in the Four Church Types

Representatives from all four church types met together to look at learning and education issues for a two day workshop. The comparative grid is the result of this process in six key areas:

Focus: the general focus of education in the congregation

Commitment level: level of commitment of the congregation to participate in education ministries

Forum: basic setting or means of experiencing education in the congregation

Participation: who takes part in education ministry

Leadership: who teaches, leads, coordinates education ministry

Impact: what impact the education ministry makes on individuals, the community of faith, the surrounding community, and the world

Retrogressive

Focus: specialized information for mission and ministry, personal development in interest areas.

Commitment: high level of commitment to growth and development in specialized areas.

Forum: small groups, ongoing classes.

Participation: widespread throughout the congregation; everyone is expected to participate in some learning option.

Leadership: a variety of leaders with expertise in specialized fields; often draws leadership from outside congregation.

Impact: high level of impact; people's behavior changed by learning; conceptual and skill learning applied to daily living/service.

Vital

Focus: integrating spiritual, theoretical, and practical knowledge in daily living and Christian service; study of Scripture, theology, cultural and sociological issues highly valued.

Commitment: high level of commitment by majority of congregation to lifelong learning; learning and discipleship are closely related.

Forum: small groups, both inside and outside the congregation; formal classes with clear objectives; integrated program.

Participation: Widespread throughout entire congregation.

Leadership: interplay of teacher/student role where almost everyone is both; a good deal of outside expertise brought in; majority of congregations see themselves in a teaching role.

Impact: high impact; lives changed, hearts transformed; people integrate faith, learning, and daily living.

Decaying

Focus: learning information about God, about the Bible, about the church. What it means to live the faithful Christian life—often in the abstract.

Commitment: sporadic; generally a small core group within the larger congregation.

Forum: Sunday school; occasional small groups for Bible study/fellowship.

Participation: limited; most adults do not share a high commitment to learning/Christian education.

Leadership: set teachers and or resident volunteers, usually with limited knowledge and experience.

Impact: people who participate enjoy it, those who don't participate don't miss it; occasional high impact on the lives of specific individuals.

Dystrophic

Focus: Learning about the Christian faith and growing in discipleship; generally aimed at individuals.

Commitment: sporadic; education is emphasized as important, but optional.

Forum: small groups, Sunday school classes; short-term study groups.

Participation: Moderate levels of participation; many people select options of personal interest; many people do not participate at all.

Leadership: set teachers and leaders with moderate experience, and often highly specialized knowledge; mostly rely on resident leaders.

Impact: unknown, for the most part; a small percentage of participants are highly motivated and behaviors are transformed; behavior unchanged for the majority.